Millennial Leadership: Everything You Need to Know

How To Understand, Retain and Motivate Gen Y Leaders

JASON E. WIGGINS, PhD

DEDICATION

All things can be done if you dream, put in the work and overcome failure. This book is dedicated to my son Hunter (my little champ), as I am truly blessed to have you as my son. Remember, anything is possible if you believe and pursue. To my wife, Luciana-You are my rock and I appreciate all that you do. I dedicate this book to all my family and friends, as I am thankful for the love and the friendships. This is just beginning of an adventurous ride.

CONTENTS

Acknowledgments   i

1 Grass Roots   1

2 Generations   11

3 Understanding Theory   17

4 Gen Y   25

5 Motivation   36

6 Workforce   50

7 Satisfaction   63

8 Millennial Leader Retention   73

9 Design   80

10 Results   84

11 Final Determinations   104

References   117

ACKNOWLEDGMENTS

I would like to acknowledge all those family, friends, and foes that have made me to the person I am today. I would not be here if it weren't for your impact in my life. I would like to acknowledge the Meridian school district in Northwest Washington State with a solid school foundation within scholastics and athletics, along with the higher academic universities I was associated in pursuing obtaining a terminal degree. I am fortunate to have a great mom (Karla Pierce) and dad (Bob Wiggins) to help me through finding my way. I, of course want to acknowledge my son Hunter for the inspiration to write this book, along with my wonderful wife (Luciana).

i

1 GRASS ROOTS

Are you looking to know more about millennial leaders and what makes them who they are? This book will provide inside perspectives of participants that are current millennial leaders. The perspective is real life and is very telling towards the largest generation in the workforce and what their work views consist of. If you are lost about how millennials operate in a leadership role, then you will likely have a greater understanding upon finishing this book. Millennial leaders are very talented and can take your business to the next level with the right mentorship and organizational structure.

Each Generation of active workers last approximately 20 years depending on the determining publication. With technology advancing and the sheer confusion from employers about millennials, or also known as Gen Y has employers and/or employees disoriented with how to approach them. The terms *Generation Y* and *millennial* are interchangeable throughout this book. Are millennial leaders that much different or is it a misconception by a generation being biased against them? A primary concern: are millennials difficult to manage or is it the lack of understanding the characteristics of the Gen Y generation. It is likely a mixture of both. However, the ensuing finish line within the book will be on point to helping each reader for a final determination of the most diverse generation of our time. The results and recommendation in this book will open up perceptions and alter idealism that some may hold true.

Millennials and the perception of millennials have help opened the job market for speakers, organization development consultants, authors, and numerous other subsidiaries to begin analyzing why or if this generation is different. Are there values different or is it the way communication is dispersed, or is there just a lack of understanding among their peers or those individuals from a far? The predominant generations currently in the workforce include the baby boomers, Gen X, and millennials. Each generation has some similarities, along with key differences. However, do not be afraid or concerned that one generation is better or more difficult to manage. The truth is as organizational development experts, the theory of how to manage each talent base is the ability to learn how to communicate to each group. Each generational group commands their own styled based on factors that were indicative of their growth years at what was experienced during those times.

Hopefully, the reason that you are reading this book today is because you would like a better understanding of millennials and particularly millennial leaders. If you are a business owner, executive, OD consultant, or a connoisseur of Gen Y leadership, then this book will demonstrate those key Gen Y leadership aspects that are on display and how we together can provide an environment that is conducive to millennial leadership. This leadership group is extremely bright and dedicated to many pursuits and if the proper guidance is provided, businesses will achieve profitability, employee engagement, and a great work environment experience within their organization. However, if millennial leaders are not treated right and properly cultivated to their expectations, then you will be right back to submitting other digital help wanted ads via Indeed, CareerBuilder, etc.

Of course, for difficult to fill positions, then you reach out to recruiters for an expansive search and this is cause for anguish due to the high finders' fee associated with hiring the recruiter generation employee, which will be discussed later. Overall, losing a leader and particularly a millennial leader is very expensive. This expensive topic will be discussed later. Therefore, together we can provide the tools that will help guide the largest generational group to guide successful businesses.

The backbone of this book was research that was based on a study of millennial leaders within a service organization who had at least five subordinates reporting to them. For the context of this study, a service industry is an industry comprised of companies that primarily earn revenue through providing intangible products and services (Service Industry). Service industry companies include transport, distribution, and food services, among other service-dominated businesses that provide services to a customer base. However, the grassroots of this research are common to retail, consumer, business to business, as it is not the industry that was so vital, but the interaction of millennials during the interviews. Ultimately, the results can be shared for most industries since the results demonstrate commonalities throughout other industries. It was telling that it was not the industry that each participant worked in that determined their outlook on the job, but it was other factors that determine their outlook and if those conditions factored into their motivation or lack thereof.

The important concepts that are indicative of the success of a Gen Y leader is the ability to motivate and retain these leaders. The rise and fall of an organization are likely in the hands of these leaders. When this is mentioned, each business owner or executive should be shaking in their heels and reaching for a bottle of gin or whatever your liquid choice is because this is scary concern. If there is an executive or business owner that has yet to focus on the retention and motivation of the Gen Y leader, then there has likely been the lack of a succession plan or visionary outlook or straight confusion. Of course, anyone reading this understand the parallels between the motivation and retaining this leadership group.

Understanding retention and motivation was critical in the development of this book. There are a significant number of motivational-based books that could provide additional posturing to how certain techniques can inspire millennials. Motivation is the force that makes individuals act negatively or positively (Islam & Ali, 2013). The theoretical definition for work motivation is inducing actions in employees while explaining the direction, duration, and intensity of their behavior (Acar, 2014; Dwivedula, Bredillet, & Müller, 2015). Other elements of work motivation are also the internal evaluation or a sense of pride for fulfilling a work commitment. Not all motivation is driven by capitalism and the all-mighty dollar. Individuals choose to work in many cases because they enjoy their type of work. As most of you know, there is a popular statement, "I have never worked a day in my life". This statement refers to loving something that you do. How many of us can say this?

With a focus on the ability to achieve results through corporate demands, it has become more important to provide methods to motivate the leadership ranks with regard to employee satisfaction in the workplace. It is becoming a necessity since organizations are knowledge based. Meaning, when an employee departs the organization, they are leaving with a wealth of knowledge and training. Again, this will cost the organization because of the cost to rehire and train for the knowledge. Therefore, it makes sense to motivate and retain your current leaders and future leaders.

During our fact-finding mission, I have included knowledge regarding how employing motivation strategies can increase satisfaction and decrease attrition of millennial leaders. Aruna and Anitha (2015) noted that common motivators such as career development, job satisfaction, style of management, nature of working style, and work environment play a role in the retention of Generation Y members. Knowledge about Generation Y leaders is lacking. A Deloitte survey from 2016 indicated that 57% of millennial leaders are likely to leave their current position by 2020 (n.d., 2016). This statement may be a concern for executive team members who manage Generation Y leaders due to the high cost of attrition in the service industry. As we are now or have recently passed this date depending when you are reading this, this trend is likely going in a negative direction if organizations do not take millennial leadership seriously. The momentum gained within the organization will be lost as the knowledge base and expertise leaves the organization due to a continued organizational disconnect with millennial leaders. It would be a mistake to think that Generation Y leaders can be managed the same way baby boomers or Generation X are being managed.

The findings of the study encapsulated the mission of social change and employee retention by providing ways to decrease Generation Y leaders' attrition rate through motivation strategies that increase job and organization satisfaction. Losing Generation Y leaders is a concern due to the cost associated with attrition and the ways retention can improve in a service organization. Using motivation strategies to increase satisfaction will likely decrease attrition for Generation Y leaders. Motivation strategies will benefit social change by decreasing attrition in Generation Y while improving executive leadership's awareness of this concern.

Key organizations who employ members of Generation Y may benefit from understanding the outcome of applying unique motivation strategies to increase satisfaction and improve retention of millennial leaders. Exploring the depth of generational challenges will help organizational owners and managers communicate approaches that will help improve the motivation, satisfaction, and retention of Generation Y leaders (Olckers & Plessis, 2012). The information obtained from the study will likely help human resources and management staff find ways to fulfill the needs of millennial leaders. According to Kleiman (2004), millennial leaders feel unsatisfied and leave their organizations earlier than former generations did, which means it is necessary to find additional solutions to conserve talent at the Generation Y leadership level.

Organizational leaders may use the results of the investigation to retain and motivate millennial leaders, which may prepare the organizational leaders to guide future generations while affecting positive social change. What we learn from retaining millennial leaders will likely also help the next generation of leaders, Generation Z. Of course, this will be a topic for another day, as this generation is or has recently entered into the workforce being fully digitized.

The concept of motivation had transcended for a significant amount of time and each philosopher or researcher has their own experiences from previous research studies. Motivation has always been a difficult topic to understand or pursue depending on the individual. The reality is all humans have different trigger points that advance their motivation tendencies. Researchers have a variety of views on work motivation that are pertinent in the workplace. According to Herzberg (1974), the problem of work motivation is the matter of people not desiring to work. I have some issues with Herzberg's theory due to too many individuals that are motivated to work and his theory is also significant to the perceived characteristics of millennials and the lack of work motivation. Ultimately, it is not the lack of work motivation, but how the means justifies the end.

There are different ways to understand motivators because each is different as mentioned early. If each of us were master motivators, we would be able to wave a magic wand to motivate others. Therefore, there would be no need for managers or a need to pursue writing this book. Unfortunately, motivation is not simple to understand or can be forced upon an unwilling participant, but there are key factors that can help. Motivators are factors that meet the needs of individuals for psychological growth, recognition, achievement, opportunity, and career advancements (Sterling & Boxall, 2013). A positive correlation often exists through work motivation between people who feel satisfied and a high employee retention rate.

The key is high retention rate of millennials when they are satisfied within the company workforce. Therefore, it is simple to keep Gen Y leaders with the organization, right? The lessons learned within research and development of millennial leader indicate that knowledge is powerful. The retention results will suggest there is a key to retaining millennial leadership within organizations by motivating at the highest level. If not, individuals will leave for other jobs for a variety of reasons. However, there are too many individuals that leave the organization because of culture, leadership and poor business practices that can be repaired, without losing key leaders.

As organization executives, there must be a constant concern for high attrition within millennials leaders because they are the current and future leaders. What is important is the understanding among concerned organizational leaders is that high attrition among Generation Y members will be a significant burden on corporations' human capital expenses. In the next few years, the Generation Y cohort will become the largest group since the baby boom generation, as baby boomers continue to leave the workforce (Eversole, Venneberg, & Crowder, 2012; Thompson & Gregory, 2012). By 2020, the members of Generation Y will comprise 46% of the workforce (Kalman, 2012). By 2030, 75% of the employees in the United States will be part of the Generation Y cohort (Meister, 2012b). Due to the workforce incorporating a high percentage of millennials, there will be a larger concern for the attrition of millennial leaders. The cost associated with Generation Y leaders leaving their respective organizations will be high. Are you prepared? If not, you will soon be.

There are many differences in managing a Generation Y leader compared to managing leaders from different generations, specifically baby boomers. Expectations have changed regarding the quality and frequency of communication (Twenge, Campbell, & Freeman, 2012). Gen Y leaders expect that communication will be an everyday part of life because this group has the desire to be treated as an equal partner versus in a hierarchal leadership. Therefore, the increase communication provides Gen Y leaders that intellectual well-being that they are a significant part of the organization. Millennial leaders have faced challenges different from previous generations, as highlighted throughout the research that included the use of technology that has influenced the growth process from early childhood into adulthood.

As previously mentioned earlier, business owners, and executives need to understand the cost of recruiting and retaining employees is high, and there is no exception for Generation Y employees. The cost of losing a Generation Y employee is between $15,000 and $25,000 (Schawbel, 2013). This associated cost could also be for a lower level hiring positions because in many executive recruitments, this cost can run between $50,000 to $75,000 depending on the position. Executive recruiters obtain 20% to 30% salary fee for finding and hiring an employee. Usually, the new hire must be hired for 6 months to one year to receive the full recruitment fee. It cannot be overstated how expensive losing a millennial leader can be. Forty-five percent of companies will experience high turnover among

Generation Y employees (Meister, 2012a).

Sixty percent of millennials search for work while employed with an organization (Hamori, Koyuncu, Cao, & Graf, 2015; Ware, 2014). This is a problem that undermines the ability to teach teamwork and mentoring when an employee has one foot out the door and are clearly disengaged at work. The cost of retention will continue to rise when millennials leave for other job opportunities. Fifty-seven percent of millennial leaders will leave their current organization by 2020 (n.d, 2016) , as I previously noted.

Researchers have studied how individuals demonstrate the characteristics of Generation Y cohorts and their deficiencies and strengths in the workplace. Nikravan (2014) posited that Generation Y members would like new jobs or assignments every 12 to 24 months. Imagine that we are always in a state of turnover, if this trend continues. How about looking at a resume that has 5-7 jobs listed in the last 10 years. This will be the norm with the current trend. Remember, we have the ability to change this, so there is hope.

Members of the Gen Y leadership group are likely to posit that this means they are sharpening their skills when leaving for other employment opportunities. While, an employer is likely to react in a negative way because they see this group as job hoppers. The thought process for organizational leaders is millennial leaders are not willing to work hard by growing organically within the organization. Some members of the baby boomer generation may state that millennials are not willing to earn their stripes. Ultimately, there are two counter arguments that are warranted and substantiated depending on the audience. This is a drastic comparison to baby boomers, who would spend a lifetime at one organization. Recent work statistics associated with Generation Y members demonstrated that Generation Y members leave their employers sooner than members of other generation.

Motivational concepts have a significant role in the ability to engage Generation Y leaders in cultivating and leading effectively by understanding their organizational culture. Being able to facilitate and motivate this group will require motivational tools that will make work enjoyable among millennial leaders and their peers. Generation Y leaders are looking for opportunities to increase their involvement through understanding their organizational culture. To understand millennial leaders, the next chapter about generations will be vital. Each generation learns from the past generation due the upbringing and overall values.

2 GENERATIONS

With a foundation about the importance of motivation and retention of millennial leaders, there also needs to be an understanding of the generations involved in our current workforce. Together, the workforce is the backbone of the community, our businesses and how we operate as a society. Individuals within each generation need to find common ground within their work habits to establish an overall understanding of the key current working groups and how they can work together.

Besides being known as Generation Y and millennials, other names for Generation Y members include nexters, Generation www, Generation E, and echo boomers (Dimitriou & Blum, 2015; Friedell, Puskala, & Villa, 2011; Zopiatis, Kapardis, & Varnavas, 2012). The universally recognizable names are Generation Y and millennials. As mentioned earlier, there are certain biases that may or may not be substantiated as some of these terms will indicate. Terms used to describe Generation Y members include lazy, impatient, self-entitled, and wanting to be a part of something meaningful (Deepthi & Baral, 2013; Zopiatis et al., 2012). Other terms used to categorize members of Generation Y are team players, ambitious, tech-savvy, and multitaskers (Beekman, 2011). There is evidence that Generation Y is different from past generations regarding their values, economies of scale, and ways they meet the work demands of their employer (Helms, 2014). Generation Y members possess qualities that can be beneficial or detrimental depending on the organizational setting.

To understand Generation Y characteristics and their applications, it is important to understand past generations. Ultimately, three generations are primarily in the workforce. A 4th generation, Gen Z has recently entered into the workforce. Members of the three generations are baby boomers, Generation X, and Generation Y. Each of these generations inhibit characteristics of the generation theory. The ideology noted in this chapter will provided serendipitous moments that can be translated well to each generation cohort.

Researchers have used generation theory to help explain the era of which each birth year is a part. The birth years of the baby boomers are between 1946 and 1965. Members of this group are heirs to the era of optimism and had experiences that included going against their parents' wishes during their early rebellious years with events such as sexual and drug experimentation. Baby boomers have a weak instinct for social discipline and a desire to infuse new values for changes (Hansen & Leuty, 2012). There was typically more resistance from baby boomers when change was occurring within organizations. This group is not a big fan of change and going outside the box, meaning it will take additional nudging and stimulation to move the needle for an anticipated result. This is a great time to pair millennials with baby boomers in projects because they can help each other. At least that is the idealism of the partnership when pursuing group activities.

This leads us to the forgotten generation, along with being the smallest generation in the overall workforce. The birth years of Generation X are between 1965 and 1979, and members of Generation X experienced the early years of the technology revolution. Many Generation X members were latchkey children because they were the children of parents who divorced or lived in poverty (Gibson, Greenwood, & Murphy, 2011; Hansen & Leuty, 2012). Many members of this generation had minimal parental guidance because their parents split up during their adolescent years. This is predominantly the first generation that lived in single-family homes compared to baby boomers and preceding generations.

Of course, one of the circumstances to having a small workforce pool was due to parents having less children due divorces within the family. Also, Gen X found themselves being responsible for their own well-being. This generation included self-governance while symbolically being known as latchkey children. Meaning, there was no coddling or participation awards among families because the support group was non-existent in most immediate families. It was quite the opposite compared to how millennials were raised. However, the Gen X group was not going to make the same 'mistakes' their parents did. The ensuing argument was is it really a mistake when there is an overabundance of cuddling that has led to the upbringing of millennials.

The birth years of the members of Generation Y or millennials were between 1980 and 2000. Researchers have targeted members of this generation as being smarter, better behaving, and more civic-minded compared to previous generations (Beekman, 2011; Gibson et al., 2011; Howe & Strauss, 1992). Millennials are willing to seek other employment opportunities if organizational leaders do not meet their preferred work conditions (E. A. Brown, Thomas, & Bosselman, 2015). Due to the size of the generation, millennials have become a forgotten cohort because they are between the Generation X and baby boomers, but will soon be larger than the baby boom generation.

Generation theory is a concept researchers use to understand the different generations in the workforce. According to generation theory, individuals' birth year affects the evolution of their cohort's view of the world (Howe & Strauss, 1992). The workforce includes a combination of age-related beliefs, work behaviors, and values as older employees prepare to exit the labor force while younger workers are planning on new careers (Combes, 2013). There has been a continuous change in the workforce from baby boomers' work ethic to the independence of Generation X and to members of Generation Y entering the workforce who are used to constant appreciation.

The overall research will likely help organizational leaders by focusing on motivational strategies that will satisfy Gen Y leaders needs through reduced attrition. Some key factors attributed to the retention factors of the Generation Y community are the social and historical differences from their predecessors. Millennials may expect to change employers as they discover ways to increase their skill levels, and they view 1 year of employment as a long-term position (Laird, Harvey, & Lancaster, 2015; Luscombe, Lewis, & Biggs, 2013). This is a significant difference in belief compared to the baby boomers because they viewed work as a lifetime position.

Knowing whether retention of the Generation Y cohort relates to motivation and having an effective means for organizational leaders to retain and motivate Generation Y leaders were essential elements in this research. Motivating employees in the workforce by enhancing human performance has continued to be a point of emphasis for employers (Okoro & Washington, 2012). Seventy-three percent of the managers surveyed in one study expressed concern about losing millennial employees (Ferri-Reed, 2014b). The inability to motivate and retain Generation Y leaders may result in loss of profits, along with the loss of valued employees. Ultimately, this will cause a large expense when human capital is lost. Keep in mind that the loss of human capital is in the same quadrant as profit loss, since the loss falls in the expense category. Businesses will need to continue to proactively cultivate and advance human performance. In return, advancing human performance will reduce the expense of human capital expenditures through minimizing the loss of millennial leaders' knowledge.

The attrition of millennial leaders is a significant concern for all executive leadership. Sixty percent of millennials leave their organization within 3 years, compared to the national average of 4.5 years for employees of all generations (Schawbel, 2013). Is it okay to have to continue to spend on the loss of human capital when the easy solution is to retain millennial leaders?

On average, millennials will have approximately 50% fewer years of tenure than their counterparts in other generations. The general problem is the high rate of current and projected attrition of future Generation Y leaders in the service sector. The specific problem addressed was the lack of knowledge and understanding in scholarly research regarding how the motivation of Generation Y leaders affects employee satisfaction while increasing employee retention factors (Luscombe et al., 2013). There is a significant opportunity to improve human capital by way of capturing the results from the noted study and then realigning these results to project goals by the organization to help retain and motivate millennials leaders.

My goal is not to bore you with in-depth research information, but there are some baseline important details that should be shared. Within the research, I explored how unique motivation strategies increased satisfaction while increasing retention among Generation Y leaders. I used a qualitative approach to capture the participants' lived experiences and to understand the experiences of millennial leaders in the service industry. The following research questions provided the context of the study to help the overall understanding of millennial leaders.

Research Question 1: What are Generation Y leaders' lived experiences and reactions when the leaders of service organizations try to motivate the teams to which they belong in the southwestern United States?

Research Question 2: What factors are causing Generation Y leaders to leave service organizations?

Research Question 3: What role does employer motivation play in the retention of Generation Y leaders in the service industry?

As a result of the qualitative research, I was able to develop a platform within the study to better prepare corporate leaders for employing motivation strategies to increase the satisfaction of Generation Y leaders and therefore decrease their attrition. The ensuing results of retention is the improvement in culture and the overall health of the organization. Fortunately, we have theorist that provide previously used instrumentation for current researchers that have a high level of standardization and respectability in the research community.

3 UNDERSTANDING THEORY

It is deemed appropriate to initiate the discussion with Maslow and Herzberg because of the similarities among the theories. Herzberg's and Maslow's theories have a connection with job satisfaction and motivation for individual growth with the ability to retain employees. When employees feel satisfied and enriched within their job capabilities, they are more likely to continue working for the same organization. Herzberg (1974) posited that satisfaction and dissatisfaction are isolated issues and acknowledged that motivation factors, if delivered correctly, increase satisfaction, but their absence does not lead to dissatisfaction (Herzberg, 1974). Herzberg described orthodox job enrichment, which includes personal growth as the key to the health of an organization and is the approach that most often results in happier employees and higher productivity (p. 71). Researchers have used Maslow's and Herzberg's theories to measure job satisfaction and motivation when observing Generation Y members. I applied Herzberg's motivation–hygiene theory on Generation Y leaders to identify the types of events that cause job satisfaction or dissatisfaction that affect the retention of this cohort.

Within the conceptual framework in this study, Maslow's hierarchy of needs included two primary motives serving as the conceptual lens to examine work motivation from basic needs to self-actualization. Maslow's hierarchy of needs displays lower order needs (physiological and safety) linked to an organization's culture. Maslow's hierarchy of needs has served as a baseline to determine employee motivation (Gupta & Tayal, 2013; Jerome, 2013). I used the link between employee productivity and employee motivation for improving employee retention. The framework led to motivational factors that increased the motivation of Generation Y leaders while leading to job satisfaction and increased employee retention.

The discussion encompassed the processes of how Maslow's hierarchy of needs is applicable to the ways members of organizations that employ Generation Y leaders can lead those leaders to the highest level of Maslow's hierarchy, which is achieving self-actualization. When self-actualization occurs, employee needs have been met, which means the retention of the employee through proper motivation has occurred. According to Jerome (2013), the role of organizational culture is to create norms and values for employee relations in certain areas to help attain self-esteem and self-actualization needs. Essential aspects of organizational benefits improve the ability to retain and motivate millennial leaders through feedback and performance reviews. This framework served as a structure to analyze millennial leaders' life experiences and the way organizational leaders can motivate and retain millennial leaders.

The concept of self-actualization is a popular term for reaching the pinnacle of your status in and out of the workforce. This fulfillment for millennial leaders is becoming more prevalent because of the personal values that are present while feeling complete when they are learning new skills, practicing social change through improvement of the environment or their favorite charity. However, the pragmatic view is associated more to the false sense of fulfillment or short-lived due to the job-hopping. The job hopping could demonstrate a fragile ego, whereas true actualization provides long-term fulfillment.

While continuing the conceptual framework, the equity theory incorporates the idea that fairness in the workplace motivates individuals. Fairness is a term that is highly associated with the workforce because of the problems it can cause. When individuals perceive their workplace is unfair, they will become unmotivated (Adams, 1965; Armache, 2012). According to Adams and Jacobsen (1964), inequality exists when the perception to ratio of the outcomes is unsatisfactory compared to the amount of effort input. The motivation for the perceived input should match the output and the reward from that specific action of input (Adams, 1965). When individuals' perception of their equity status increases, their motivation will increase.

The basis of Adams's equity theory is the difference between inequality and equality and the perceived value of the input put forth. Adams and Jacobsen (1964) explained that whenever two individuals exchange anything, there is always a possibility that either party will deem the exchange inequitable. Individuals consider inequality to exist when the ratio of input to the ratio of output is unequal compared to others who work in different organizations involved with the same level of ratio of input to level of output. Individuals are less likely to feel concern when their efforts are rewarded compared to the similar efforts of others.

Adams's equity theory was applicable in my research through the involvement of millennial leaders who developed their motivation and job satisfaction through their efforts and outputs. When comparing others who work in similar positions within their organization or outside their organization, individuals want fair compensation regardless of the organization. When inequality occurs, there is a decrease in motivation and effort (Adams & Jacobsen, 1964). The outcome of how much effort millennial leaders put forth will determine what equity in return will be satisfactory.

Another noted prominent theory known as Vroom's expectancy theory affects the wants and desires of individuals through outcomes. Researchers have used expectancy theory to explain work phenomena that include job satisfaction, work behavior, and occupational preferences (Chou & Pearson, 2012; Vroom, 1964). According to the expectancy theory, the amount of effort put into a performance will translate to obtaining positive outcomes or rewards (Hema Malini & Washington, 2014; Malik, Butt, & Choi, 2015). The effect of expectancy theory includes acting as a predictor of how someone will react after they have acknowledged the outcome (Malik et al., 2015; Vroom, 1964). The expectancy theory can help with determining how people can feel motivated to claim the rewards desired.

The discussion of the expectancy theory was applicable to how an outcome can satisfy and motivate millennial leaders through the outcome. Expectancy theory identifies valence as a requirement for any reward to have an effect on others (Malik et al., 2015). Valence refers to how an individual perceives the value of expected rewards. The expected rewards can be different for millennial leaders, depending on the outcome desired. This framework helped illustrate how to retain millennial leaders by finding the desired rewards to improve their satisfaction and motivation.

Employers who employ Generation Y members will benefit from understanding how to retain and motivate millennial leaders. Therefore, understanding millennial leaders will be the likelihood health or slow dissolvement of a business. However, exploring the depth of generational challenges will support organizational owners and managers by communicating approaches that will improve the motivation, attraction, and retention of Generation Y leaders (Olckers & Plessis, 2012). The information obtained from the study may support human resources and management staff members finding new ways to gratify the needs of millennial leaders. According to Kleiman (2004), millennial leaders feel unsatisfied and leave their companies earlier than members of former generations did, which means it is necessary to find additional solutions to conserve talent at the Generation Y leadership level. Organizational leaders may use the results of the investigation to retain and motivate millennial leaders, which may prepare the organizational leaders to guide future generations while effecting positive social change.

The qualitative approach aligned with the choice of a conceptual framework that consisted of Maslow's hierarchy of needs, Vroom's expectancy theory, Adams's equity theory, and Herzberg's two-factory theory. The qualitative study involved delving into the lived experiences of the participants who indicated their needs and satisfaction, which helped determine the motivation techniques required and the potential to increase the retention of Generation Y leaders. Obtaining individual feedback from the participants is vital because this provides first-hand knowledge versus an author stating opinions versus facts.

As we move into some of the key research aspects, there are assumptions that need to be determined prior to a study being completed. Without this foundation, a study will have no parameters to define the research. Therefore, the research about millennial leaders will be valid in a way that promotes a valid conclusion while assumptions about the study are predetermined. Assumptions in a study can be partially out of a researcher's control, but the study would be pointless without them (Simon, 2011). Our purpose is to provide a valid foundation for a better understanding of Gen Y leaders.

The first assumption in the study was Generation Y leader participants would respond honestly during the interviews. Of course, this should be a given. The expectation was the interview process would yield data that provided significant insight into the thoughts and attitudes of

Generation Y leaders. The participants included individuals willing to participate with the option to withdraw at any time. It was important to know participants were not being forced to participate, if the felt any discomfort.

The second assumption was that the Generation Y leaders would be working full-time for their organization while completing the interview process. Through the second assumption, I was able to acknowledge that the participants were full-time employees and that they completed the interview process. As mentioned before, the participants had the ability to opt out at any time and for any reason. Ultimately, all the participants were generous with their time.

The last assumption was that a qualitative approach was the most appropriate approach. The study included the ability to understand the real-life experiences of the participants as millennial leaders. This approach likely helped yield data from the participants' lived experiences while extracting information to develop relevant themes that best identified the phenomenon studied. With the assumptions in place, I was confident that the research would provide conclusive detail about the most interesting generation of our time.

The parameters consists of the following elements to ensure that all participants were equal to provide a valid study. The results of this study are generalizable to millennial leaders who (a) work in the service industry, (b) work in the southwestern United States, and (c) have at least five subordinates reporting to them. Another outcome was that there is less concern about blue-collar or temporary employees than about white-collar employees due to the focus of the study on Generation Y leaders.

As part of the research, I documented the lived experience of Generation Y leaders regarding how motivation has a direct correlation with retention in organizations in the United States. The research about

Generation Y leaders was unique because there was a lack of information about why members of this group are leaving their career positions early. Therefore, members of organizations that employ Generation Y leadership will likely benefit from understanding the underlying specifics of retaining and motivating this cohort. The information provided may serve to encourage individuals in management and human resource personnel to cater to the needs of millennial leaders and reduce attrition within their organizations. Some readers may state, "What, more than we already have"? Let's keep in mind that if the right tools are utilized, then organizations will be poised to make leaps and bounds to reaching their goals due to retaining valued team leaders.

Researchers investigating generational challenges may inform management personnel about ways to help motivate, retain, and attract millennial leaders (Olckers & Plessis, 2012). According to Tulgan (2009), it is imperative to find alternative solutions to keep talent at the Generation Y leadership level because these leaders are leaving organizations earlier than past generations did. I sought to help organizational leaders retain and motivate Generation Y leaders through this study to prepare Generation Y leaders to lead future generations while making positive social change.

I sought to discover unique motivation strategies that improve satisfaction while also improving retention among millennial leaders. Specifically, senior leaders have found it difficult to motivate and improve retention with the current methods. Therefore, leaders must have an effective strategic plan for improving motivation techniques, increasing satisfaction, and improving retention rates for millennial leaders.

Human resource practitioners and educators may benefit from these findings to understand what motivates millennials leaders and what strategies are suitable to recruit and prevent unnecessary turnover. RecruitiFi (2014), a crowdsourced talent acquisition platform, indicated that

83% of millennials understand that job-hopping on the resume has the potential to reflect poorly on applicants; however, 86% indicated that the potential of a poor reflection would not prevent them from pursuing other opportunities. The research findings are likely to improve social change for senior leaders, educators, and human resources practitioners by using motivation techniques to recruit, motivate, and improve retention.

Understanding the problems of the Generation Y cohort and finding possible solutions to retain and motivate a group within the cohort is important in promoting employee retention and job satisfaction among millennials. Evidence exists that the Generation Y cohort is much different from previous generations. A key determination includes how leadership and motivation affect the experiences of Generation Y leaders with regard to their satisfaction and retention. Organizational leaders are aware of the financial implications that millennial turnover can cause to their organizations. The cost to employers is the loss of valuable information when employees leave, as well as the cost of replacing employees.

4 GEN Y

To understand the influence of motivation and retention on Generation Y leaders, I explored literature for information related to generational differences, retention, and motivation and the overall evaluation of millennial leadership. A significant amount of information exists about different motivational concepts, but researchers have not produced adequate documentation to demonstrate the impact of motivation and its effect on the retention of Generation Y employees. The focus of the information presented included how to retain and motivate members of the Generation Y leadership cohort.

Identifying the costs of retaining Generation Y leaders and their individual talents is vital in understanding how organizations can succeed. There is a need to understand this generation, which will soon be the largest generational group in U.S. history as baby boomers leave the workforce, with approximately 80 million members (Goudreau, 2013). This qualitative study included the motivational influences that affect the retention of millennial leaders within the southwestern United States.

Generational differences in the workplace comprise the entire history on how individuals in leadership positions motivate, train, and recruit their employees. Demographics regarding work ethics, values, and ways to motivate others have changed. For the first time, four generations are working together, so it is essential to understand each generation and the ways members of Generation Y affect how organizations may operate in the future (Hansen & Leuty, 2012; Putre, 2013). For example, many organizational leaders have created favorable working conditions by incorporating technology and open workspaces that are conducive to informal meetings (Kilber et al., 2014). The change in workload and job status for members of Generation X and millennials is significant, as members of the second largest cohort, baby boomers, continue to retire in large numbers, and these two groups will succeed them in leadership positions.

Generation Y is a label that includes individuals born between 1980 and 2000. Millennials are the offspring of baby boomers and early members of Generation X, and many members of Generation X were guilty of nepotism with their millennial children. Millennials' parents, who are participation oriented and communicative, nurtured their children (Dimitriou & Blum, 2015). Generation Y is the largest cohort, at close to 80 million members (Cahill & Sedrak, 2012). There are approximately 76 million baby boomers and nearly 60 million members of Generation X in the workforce (Cahill & Sedrak, 2012). The generational tension among employees is real because of the different values experienced in the workplace, so it is difficult to determine the best way to manage the Generation Y workforce. However, the results of the research are notable and useful while helping improve and retain millennial leaders.

As baby boomers continue to exit the workforce at a constant rate, members of Generation X and millennials are continuing to advance in the workforce. Millennials will comprise approximately 75% of the global workforce by 2020, and then 50% of the labor pool by 2030 (Ismail & Lu, 2014; Kuhl, 2014). According to Meister (2012a), 91% of millennials will stay with a company less than 3 years. However, in a survey of postsecondary students, 50% of millennial participants indicated they would prefer to spend their career with one organization (Schweitzer & Lyons, 2010). Millennials have intentions to stay employed with one organization, but leadership's inability to retain them is a concern.

Experts who study Generation Y have labeled the members of this generation as job hoppers. They are more racially and ethnically diverse than older adults and willing to take more chances than older generations (Stowe, 2013). The members of the millennial generation do not mind leaving a job if they are not gaining the skills needed to move ahead in their career (Hamori et al., 2015). Members of the Generation Y cohort have taken a unique path with their employment endeavors, as data have shown that compensation is not the primary driver for this new working generation.

Millennials are looking for fulfilling opportunities to make a difference in society. This goes back to the likely falsehoods to reaching self-actualization early on without experiencing a full workforce lifecycle. Millennials are optimistic, hardworking, and civic-minded, unable to handle criticism, and known for being self-absorbed (Dimitriou & Blum, 2015; Korzynski, 2013). Millennials are the most civic-minded group since the silent generation, and while members of other generations tended to be more individualistic, millennials are less individualistic (Twenge et al., 2012). However, they live with their parents longer in comparison to previous generations, and moves away from their parents' house prior to the age of 27 were not permanent for more than half of the millennial population, as 54.6% moved back to their parents' home at some point before reaching age 27 (Dey & Pierret, 2014). Forty-four percent of millennials who returned home did not have a job, 25% of millennials who lived at home worked, while the remaining 31% had yet to enter the workforce

(Goodman, 2015). Generation X parents exemplified children for their accomplishments and participation in their prime adolescent years because of the differences in how their parents raised them. Yes, Gen X is part of the problem, as well as part of the solution due to their latchkey status during their prominent growth years.

Members of Generation Y have experienced many things for the first time, including being the first generation to have access to the Internet during their early youth. The millennials grew up during a time of economic prosperity and built strong bonds with their parents (Holt, Marques, & Way, 2012). The millennial generation is the first generation to adopt social media as the primary way to connect and acquire information from others, which changed the dynamics of communication (Paulin, Ferguson, Jost, & Fallu, 2014). The constructs of social media have presented new challenges that no previous generation members have faced while affecting their social well-being.

Understanding the Generation Y status can likely be demonstrated through their extensive knowledge of computers compared to previous generations. It can be noted that a Geneneration Y user is likely more capable to diagnose a computer issue versus other generations. Being the inaugural generation for the adaptation within the use of computers on a consistent basis provided millennials with confidence to communicate using technology on a social media platform (Kapoor & Solomon, 2011). Millennials' relationship with technology is the most conspicuous difference between millennials and the previous generations (Eastman, Lyer, Liao-Troth, Williams, & Griffin, 2014; Farrell & Hurt, 2014). Prior to Generation Y, people communicated face-to-face rather than electronically. Members of the millennial generation have views that are different from past generations because of the advancements made in technology and the widespread incorporation of technology into their daily lives.

The considerable amount of diversity between the four current generation cohorts is likely to continue in the future, although very few members of the silent generation remain in the workforce. Millennials have experienced a different upbringing than their predecessors due to the many technological advancements (Eastman et al., 2014; Festing & Schafer, 2014). The years following millennials' birth were a technological revolution, unlike what members of Generation X experienced in their early adolescent years.

The Generation Y cohort has demonstrated competitive tendencies among peers. Millennials desire achievement, happiness, and fulfillment, and they believe they can achieve these in the workplace (Farrell & Hurt, 2014). They are a self-confident group and are sure of their competence because they have grown up in a structured environment (Goudreau, 2013). Millennials' confidence, which comes from their upbringing in an everyone-wins culture, can cause some social concerns when nothing goes according to plan.

Millennials understand the difference in finding value in the workplace compared to previous generations. Cross-generational survey data supported a description of millennials as increasingly materialistic and extrinsic while placing a high value on image and money (Paulin et al., 2014). Strauss and Howe predicted that millennials would become a more socially conservative, community-involved group compared to previous generations (as cited in Taylor, 2014). Millennials tend to respect authority without questioning their leadership (Lancaster & Stillman, 2002). With the family being such a large part of millennial children's growth, they have a significant amount of respect. In many cases, families continue to protect millennials from failure by providing constant support, which can be a concern when millennials first face challenging situations in the workforce.

The members of the Generation Y cohort have mastered the ability to multitask, and many of them believe they can handle more than one job at once. Millennials posited that by continuing to job hop, they will not remain static in their career progression. They believe they will continue to acquire different skills for advancement while having 15 to 20 jobs during their professional life span (Meister, 2012a). According to research from the Bureau of Labor Statistics, millennials change jobs every 1.8 years (Ware, 2014). In many cases, millennials do not feel that they need to pay their societal dues, as they expect others to hand them status rather than having to achieve the status within an organization (Meister, 2012a). Not all the data collected indicated that millennials do not need to work their way up with an organization, but the majority of the data searched had similar suggestions.

Members of the Generation Y cohort find transparency in an organization and positive attributes when they share information about the organization through ensuring open communication, providing feedback, and involving employees in the decision-making process when applicable. Members of Generation Y need flexibility and constant feedback (Kauri, 2013; Solnet & Kralj, 2011). If millennials are learning new skills, regardless of the tenure of the job, they will likely continue to demand additional promotions and increased compensation because of their work experiences and newfound knowledge. Members of the millennial generation grew up with protective parents who helped enforce their confidence by creating self-confidence and urging them to pursue their dreams (Rikleen, 2014). Therefore, if millennials see their organization as transparent and leadership as significant resources for advancement, then they will likely see the value of staying with the organization for a prolonged period.

Organizational leaders encourage managers to find enthusiastic, young, promising employees who challenge the inflexibility of the standard workday, dress codes, and employee–supervisor relationships (Dimitriou &

Blum, 2015). Members of Generation X and millennials have lost their faith in the organizations that employ them and have put their trust in their individual bosses. In many cases, employees do not leave organizations, they leave their bosses. This statement goes back to why you are likely reading this book. There is a thirst for a better understanding on how we can work to motivate and retain our millennial leaders. Dissatisfaction with their bosses is the top reason members of the younger generations terminate their employment prematurely. Generation Y employees desire to work for the right leader or they will change jobs (Marston, 2007). Millennials' values have changed compared to the generations before them, and they are not willing to persevere with an employer if they are not able to find the path to success.

Generation Y members entering the workforce present different opportunities and challenges to organizations. Members of the Generation Y cohort want to be part of an energetic and innovative organization that values their opinion (Lowe, Levitt, & Wilson, 2011). The baby boomers believed in rising to the top of their respective organization and climbing the corporate ladder. Promotional opportunities were important to the members of the baby boom generation, as their plan was to develop employment stability, settle down, and raise a family. This idea is contrary to millennials' beliefs, as they take nothing for granted (Meister, 2012a). Members of the millennial cohort demand opportunities from their work environment and will leave their organization if they do not feel satisfied with their career progression within the organization.

Generation Y members want to learn new skills and need regular feedback, which is critical to their personal and professional development. Members of Generation Y are quick learners and have the capability to acclimate to modern technology improvements while incorporating them into their daily lives (Dimitriou & Blum, 2015). They are willing to sacrifice a long-term position to learn valuable skills that will enhance their career opportunities. To succeed, millennials need to know that the organization supports their goals.

An indicator for the success of an organization is the ability to retain valuable employees. With Generation X leading the way in job transfers, the millennials have begun to follow. Unlike the baby boomers, who would spend a career with the same employer, Generation Y members want to know how they can advance and how organizational leaders decide salaries. Millennials value mission-driven organizations whose leaders appreciate their contributions (Saratovsky & Feldmann, 2013). A significant obstacle for organizational leaders to overcome is what methods will result in the positive retention of Generation Y members.

Let us start discussing the elephant in the room: Employee turnover is a cause of lost production for management personnel, as expenses for hiring and training new recruits increase, and inexperienced workers must perform essential jobs, which leads to a reduction in productivity. Employee turnover is an expensive and time-consuming endeavor. A cautious estimation of the cost of turnover is 30% of a yearly salary, and as high as 250% for hard-to-replace positions (Hester, 2013). As companies are responsible for 50% of all turnover, organizational leaders must look at the competence and expertise leaving the organization (Lancaster & Stillman, 2002). As mentioned previously, employees leave their direct supervisor, not the organization, for other opportunities. Supervisors must have outstanding skills to be able to communicate and connect with the Generation Y talent. Improving supervisory skills will reduce the cost of training, improve productivity, and retain talented employees within an organization.

A critical skill for retaining Generation Y members is the ability to help engagement between the organization, supervision, and employee.

Human resource personnel and traditional media outlets have criticized this generation because of how parents raised their Generation Y children (Kellison, Yu Kyoum, & Magnusen, 2013). Generation Y members hold values that are similar to those held by traditionalists, such as being patriotic, valuing home and family, and having a sense of morality. Millennials desire a high level of pay and status while putting forth minimal effort, which has led to characterizing them as high maintenance or needy.

Millennials dislike micromanagement and desire immediate feedback on their performance. Micromanaging Gen Y leaders is likely one of the fastest steps for them to pursue other opportunities. Millennials respond well to a coaching management style while they develop skills to keep them up-to-date (Lowe et al., 2011). This style highlights collaboration and equality between employer and employee. Millennial leaders demand freedom and flexibility that allow them to act as equals to their supervisors while valuing organizations that offer less restrictive schedules and flextime (Kellison et al., 2013). Increasing millennials' skills is not the same as providing them an increased workload that they do not find challenging.

The influencers in millennials' lives who have a can-do attitude have driven the millennials to succeed. Generation Y members prefer their leaders to treat them as partners in the organization through a flat hierarchy (Kellison et al., 2013; Lowe et al., 2011). With the right mentoring, millennials can possess the ability and attitude to succeed at a high level. To engage Generation Y members properly, managers will need to forego the boss mentality to practice mentoring and coaching. Organizational leaders motivate millennials by providing the tools to help them become more productive and creative. According to NAS Recruitment Innovation (2014), Generation Y members look for organizations to provide several tools for engagement: (a) clearly stated goals, (b) frequent contact with supervision, (c) challenges, (d) regular feedback, (e) opportunities to work in teams, (f) seeing work make a difference, and (g) receiving pay for what they do and not for how long it takes them.

Many Generation Y members see challenges as motivation for increased performance. Millennials also hope to have a positive influence on the organization and make a positive change in the world (Holt et al., 2012). Millennials have grown up achieving awards for participation, and they enjoy being part of a group that is successful. The millennial cohort requires a certain amount of collaboration that is imperative for the team, as they have experienced a team atmosphere since their early childhood years, and this is vital to their success.

Incentivizing is a concept that provide a level of excitement because we all like to know what is in it for me. However, different incentives mean different things to certain groups. Generation Y members are different from members of previous cohorts, as various incentives motivate them. According to Hewlett, Sumberg, and Sherbin (2009), the best types of rewards and compensation include (a) working with great employees, (b) accommodating work arrangements, (c) achieving advancement opportunities, (d) receiving recognition from senior management within the organization, and (e) having opportunities for new experiences and challenges.

Millennials want to work for a company that has values like their own. In addition to what is listed above, employers must listen to their employees and provide them the chance to contribute and communicate the company's mission and values (Kilber et al., 2014). The key to millennializing an organization's workforce is to inspire employees to deliver their best while being innovative (Ferri-Reed, 2014b). Researchers have discovered that members of Generation Y want to be part of the decision-making process as much as possible. This does not mean that we must provide ownership in the company. However, it does mean that company stakeholders need to communicate and collaborate different ideas to determine the overall success of the project. Millennials always worked together in teams growing up, so they believe that they are good collaborators and can contribute to an organization's success.

5 MOTIVATION

Many motivational theories affect individuals through their emotional intelligence. Emotional Intelligence is thought to be a strong characteristic for millennials and is important to address. The two primary types of motivators that Herzberg theorized about were intrinsic and extrinsic motivation. Intrinsic motivation is an experience in self-motivation, while extrinsic motivation is about how outside influences affect a person's well-being. In addition to the internal and external motivation types, other academic experts focused on work motivation, including McGinley, Weese, Thompson, and Leahy (2011), who studied millennials and other generation cohorts. Another theorist who affected job enrichment is McGregor, who made a substantial impact on, and influenced, attitudes at work. However, organizational leaders have embraced Maslow's hierarchy of needs and Herzberg's two-factor theory.

Motivation is a crucial indicator for getting individuals excited and committed to performing their work at a high level. Managements' commitment to the employee is finding opportunities to expose their talents. Goal setting is a procedural method that serves to encourage employees to help them understand their responsibilities (Sultan, 2012). The goal-setting theory consists of work motivation that connects the core characteristic of objectives with outcomes such as individual performance while offering goal commitment, self-efficacy, and feedback (Berson, Halevy, Shamir, & Erez, 2015). Specific goals lead to an increasing level of commitment and a more individual focus (Berson et al., 2015). The aspects of job enrichment and goal setting noted above are necessary for a discussion on the Generation Y cohort.

As indicated in an earlier chapter, Maslow is a key figure in the principles of motivation. It is very uncommon when motivation and Abraham Maslow are not intertwined. Maslow wrote an article titled "A Theory of Human Motivation" in 1943, in which he covered the idea of human beings needing more than one act of motivation while having the drive of an animal. Motivation theory is not interchangeable with behavior theory. Types of behavior are usually motivated and revolve around cultural, biological, and situational aspects (Maslow, 1943). Maslow was an expert in the field of motivation and one of the key figures in the concept of motivation. Effective leaders who can identify motivational traits in employees will have more success than individuals who have difficulty understanding emotions. Maslow's hierarchy of needs is a process that can help leaders become more transparent and achieving the respect of the workforce.

Maslow's hierarchy of needs is one of the most identified theories relating to how employees see their own life cycle. Maslow's work on self-actualization, which appears at the top of the needs pyramid, stemmed from work by Jung, who described the process toward achieving self-realization (Rozuel, 2011). Maslow noted individuals' conscious and unconscious combine to form their personality, but a lack of education or experience can interrupt the formation process (Ivtzan, Gardner, Bernard, Sekhon, & Hart, 2013). Researchers have integrated and amended Maslow's hierarchy for practical applications while covering diverse topics. Maslow's five-level hierarchy comprises the highest-level need to the lowest level need, which are self-actualization, esteem, love, safety, and physiological.

Maslow's hierarchy of needs is helpful for understanding individuals' needs at work for determining how to satisfy them. Maslow warned that depriving needs would possibly influence negative behaviors and attitudes (Ozguner & Ozguner, 2014). Maslow aimed to explain employees' personal development needs and human motivation. Other factors involved can interrupt internal and external motivation and stifle the development process. Maslow (1943) noted that approximately 85% of physiological needs, 70% of safety requirements, 50% of love needs, 40% of self-esteem needs, and 10% self-actualization needs satisfy the average individual. These percentages are what an average individual would consider the minimum satisfaction within the hierarchy of needs scale. Maslow's hierarchy of needs in Figure 3 includes the needs and what they entail.

The steps in Maslow's hierarchy consist of having basic needs met, such as food, water, and oxygen. Maslow noted that physiological needs are nutrients, chemicals, and the internal or environment circumstances required for the human body to persevere; a prolonged absence of these needs could lead to psychological stress or physical death (Sundriyal & Kumar, 2014; Taormina & Gao, 2013). Maslow's hierarchy consists of steps that lead to the highest degree of self-actualization after the satisfaction of those needs has occurred. The satisfaction of all the psychological, safety, love, and esteem needs must occur in order to achieve self-actualization. However, if individuals have satisfied all their needs, then restlessness and discontent will soon develop unless they are doing the type of activity they enjoy (Maslow, 1943). Individuals who have satisfied needs are likely happy and have a positive emotional state.

The desired state of being is to achieve self-actualization when an individual achieves success. Self-actualization is a mental awareness that a goal or an achievement has been successful. However, individuals must meet other objectives and needs before they reach self-actualization. Maslow (1970) noted that if all the needs remain unsatisfied, and physiological needs overcome the individual, the other requirements will be unimportant. Regardless of any other needs in the hierarchy, an individual will seek food above all. The urge to do anything else will subside if hunger and thirst remain unsatisfied (Maslow, 1970). Humans have the desire to improve, which is why after individuals achieve success, they continue to move forward to complete the next quest. However, the satisfaction of basic needs must occur first.

Physiological needs are the essential elements required first because they are necessary for survival. It is difficult to move up Maslow's hierarchy of needs when there is a lack of access to basic needs such as food and water. Maslow indicated physiological needs take precedence because they must be relatively satisfied or the other level of needs will not stimulate the behavior within the hierarchy of needs (Noltemeyer, Bush, Patton, & Bergen, 2012; Ozguner & Ozguner, 2014). One approach to shroud the higher motivations and have a nonlevel playing field is to make an individual exceedingly thirsty or hungry. After a person overcomes the hunger and thirst obstacles, other needs arise and so on (Maslow, 1943). The focus is on fulfilling the physiological needs first to enable an individual to advance to other requirements that include security, social, esteem, and self-actualizing needs. After the physiological needs are satisfied, an individual no longer concentrates on the basic needs. That individual will then focus on satisfying other needs within the hierarchy.

Physiological needs are the needs that are vital for living, including air, sleep, food, and water; other requirements will follow in each level of importance. Unfulfilled lower needs dominate behavior and thinking until an individual satisfies those needs (Noltemeyer et al., 2012). Maslow indicated these are the best basic requirements in the hierarchy. Security requirements include basic safety and security, such as shelter, safe neighborhood, health care, and steady employment (Wenling, 2012). Maslow noted that one level may take priority at any one time, and it is likely that multiple needs motivate an individual concurrently (Noltemeyer et al., 2012). After individuals have satisfied their security and physiological needs, they can move up the hierarchy of needs, depending on the precedence at the time.

Fulfilling security and physiological needs is imperative to move up Maslow's triangle. Social needs include love, affection, and belonging (Milheim, 2012). Maslow noted these needs are less basic than physiological and security needs. Social needs consist of romantic and friend relationships, along with participation in social, religious, and community groups. Esteem needs are those in which individuals reflect on their self-esteem, personal worth, recognition, and personal accomplishment.

The fundamental principle of the hierarchy of needs appears as a triangle and contains different steps. Maslow (1970) admitted that the triangle might not be as rigid as first thought, as some individuals believe love and belonging are not significant and will not be satisfied. When individuals believe love and belonging are not significant, they are overcompensating for the lack of love and belonging (Maslow, 1970). Individuals may have different aspirations in life that do not correlate with Maslow's hierarchy of needs. Millennials who aspire to be successful are more likely looking to attain self-actualization.

Attaining self-actualization can be the aspect that motivates individuals to succeed because of internal motivation or external motivation. Self-actualization encompasses the involvement of individuals realizing their personal growth who want to fulfill their potential but do not focus on what others think about them (Maslow, 1970). The intent to reach self-actualization involves striving to achieve goals by incorporating the lower levels of Maslow's hierarchy of needs theory (H. Liu & Han, 2013). Many theorists have challenged the validity and different perspectives of Maslow's hierarchy of needs, and a compelling argument is that individuals do not need to complete each step before they attain a higher status. Maslow indicated in subsequent research that individuals could meet needs simultaneously.

Individuals may satisfy the need for esteem even if they have not completely fulfilled safety, although this is an ongoing topic of debate. The validity and use of Maslow's hierarchy remains debatable, with critics arguing that Maslow's hierarchy is nontestable and lacks empirical validation (Dye, Mills, & Weatherbee, 2005). For example, Maslow's hierarchy of needs theory has received criticism for gender bias while others have stated that it is for both sexes (Taormina and Gao, 2013). Maslow's research is some of the most studied, in part because of the controversial material about which scholars have different opinions. The emergence of new information extended the original pyramid to include an additional level.

Prior to his death, Maslow identified a sixth level of need, above self-actualization, that leads to an aspiration for personal success at all costs. The majority of individuals do not know as much about this addition to the hierarchy as about the other levels. Self-transcendence is the sixth level of human motivation located above self-actualization, at which point people aspire to foster a purpose beyond the self and to experience a communion beyond the confines of an individual through great achievements (Guess, 2014; Koltko-Rivera, 2006). According to Venter (2012), self-transcendence goes beyond individual needs, as an all-encompassing mind-set, common objective, and concerted accountability for their organization represented leaders. Maslow created the sixth part of the pyramid because he realized that the transcendence of opinion by others, not an egotistical presence, represents a completely established individual (Venter, 2012). The self-transcendence level became an important concept that expanded Maslow's original experiences.

After Maslow's death, self-transcendence began to be more than a favorite buzzword that emphasized high status. However, issues of corruption and turmoil started to occur when the leaders of organizations began to abuse their leadership and became self-serving, such as Ken Lay at Enron and former stockbroker Bernie Madoff (Venter, 2012). Organizational leaders became conscious of how leaders are running their business beyond profits (Niaz, 2011). After the corporate corruptions that occurred, key members of organizations began to focus on the ethical and moral values needed to run a successful organization within the guidelines of corporate responsibility.

Maslow felt the need to make a difference in society, and he described the hierarchy as a pathway to educate both males and females. Moreover, Maslow felt that organizational leaders needed to generate opportunities within the organization that were conducive to employees achieving self-actualization (Dye et al., 2005). After employees achieve self-actualization, they feel inspired by needs not yet fulfilled, and after they have satisfied those needs, the needs no longer serve as motivators (Taormina & Gao, 2013). Maslow envisioned a society that encouraged the growth and self-actualization of all individuals. Encouraging growth is likely to help eradicate inadequate services and faulty products.

Maslow indicated that individuals must demand basic needs within the hierarchy before they can reach success within the hierarchy. Maslow's greatest concern appeared to be a valueless society conceptualized when adults underestimate the importance of values within society (Taormina & Gao, 2013). Maslow asserted that an individual requires meaningful work to self-actualize (Taormina & Gao, 2013). Maslow supported individuals being able to recognize success through motivation and self-perspective so they can achieve self-actualization if they invest the time. Herzberg's two-factor theory serves as a different way to look at satisfying needs, as well as to review the importance of dissatisfied needs.

The essential understanding of Herzberg's two-factor theory is the distinct correlation between individuals in the workplace feeling satisfied or unsatisfied and the ways the two are synonymous with the term's hygiene and motivation factors. The terms two-factor theory, motivation–hygiene theory, and Herzberg's motivation theory are interchangeable. Herzberg developed the theory that work motivation entails two elements, intrinsic and extrinsic motivation, that affect employees' productivity because of their satisfaction (Damij, Levnajic, Rejec, & Sukland, 2015). The following job aspects can lead to dissatisfaction: job security, the status of an employee, procedures, regulations, salary, and working conditions (Kulchmanov & Kaliannan, 2014). The hygiene factors are imperative to the viability of the job and to an individual's perception.

The second factor is intrinsic motivation, which will help satisfy employees when their job meets needs such as achievement, advancement, responsibility, and work and growth opportunities (Kulchmanov & Kaliannan, 2014). When these motivation factors are present, then employees experience motivation and encouragement to exceed production requirements, which leads to personal self-development (Kulchmanov & Kaliannan, 2014). The underlying success in motivation is inducing people to perform things that they may not do without extra incentive. Organizational leaders need to be aware of job dissatisfaction that can alienate employees and need to find ways to help with job satisfaction and to know how motivation is essential to the organization's success.

Herzberg incorporated the motivation to work and ways such motivation affected employees in the workforce. In *The Motivation to Work*,

Herzberg solicited 203 managers and other professionals to answer a series of questions about when they felt satisfied and dissatisfied with their jobs (Smith & Shields, 2013). Interviewers identified two major factors affecting dissatisfaction and satisfaction: motivation and hygiene. The factors served to elevate the idea that each factor is a key determinant in how any employee views work.

Researchers have supported the idea that motivation factors closely relate to job satisfaction. Herzberg noted that a work-related role and the competence to achieve one's need for self-actualization would impact job satisfaction (Smith & Shields, 2013). The definition of satisfaction is "a positive emotional state resulting from the appraisal of one's job or job experience" (D. Liu, Mitchell, Lee, Holtom, & Hinkin, 2012, p. 1362). Herzberg urged organizational leaders to enrich employees' jobs to enhance their satisfaction in their job (Islam & Ali, 2013). Herzberg was a pioneer in understanding employee satisfaction.

Psychological growth is an integral part of individuals learning and creating the ability to succeed in their chosen professions. Herzberg (1974) posited there are two types of achievement: satisfaction with motivator forces and satisfaction with hygiene factors. Herzberg also documented that all motivator factors involve psychological growth and hygiene factors include psychological and physical pain avoidance. The six stages of psychological growth are (a) knowing more, (b) understanding, (c) effectiveness in ambiguity, (d) real growth, and (e) creativity (Herzberg, 1974). Herzberg had valid points that generated interest and additional studies to investigate job satisfaction and job dissatisfaction that may be advantageous to millennials as they enter the workforce.

The ensuing argument is that it is counterproductive to use hygiene factors as a motivator. Herzberg initially developed the theory to explain sources of dissatisfaction and satisfaction in the workplace in a variety of fields (R. Lacey, Kennett-Hensel, & Manolis, 2015). Ngima and Kyongo (2013) noted leaders should not use hygiene factors to motivate employees and then expect them not to feel bored with their work. If leaders cannot make a job enjoyable through job enrichment, then it is reasonable to use bonuses, bribes, and reward contingencies to motivate employees (Ngima & Kyongo, 2013). According to R. Lacey et al. (2015), when hygiene factors are sufficient, they may appease employees but not satisfy them. However, when hygiene factors are inadequate, employees feel dissatisfied.

There are better ways to motivate employees than monetarily. Managers should not attempt to motivate employees by offering a bonus, better pay, or benefits when they can offer interesting work, better training, and more responsibility (Herzberg, 1974). The important distinction is that hygiene factors contribute to dissatisfaction, not satisfaction, whereas motivator factors contribute to satisfaction, not dissatisfaction (Tuch & Hornbaek, 2015). The motivational factors listed below can help employees to have a positive work experience and a positive attitude to be successful in their organization. Hygiene and motivation have a distinct relationship that can be mutually beneficial when understood.

There are many commonalities between Maslow's hierarchy of needs and Herzberg's two-factor theory. Maslow suggested that managers should assign particular needs to various levels of achievement, which drives behaviors associated with work attitudes, whereas Herzberg asserted that an individual's desires that affect work attitudes can be extrinsically and intrinsically motivated (Udechukwu, 2009). Unlike Maslow's theory, Herzberg's motivation–hygiene theory indicated that job dissatisfaction and job satisfaction are the results of different causes. Dissatisfaction is the outcome of hygiene *factors,* and happiness depends on the motivator (Damij et al., 2015). When hygiene factors are absent or inadequate, then employee satisfaction is likely low.

The two-factor hygiene–motivation theory consists of characteristics that lead to dissatisfaction and willingness to withdraw from an employer. Therefore, when pay is not satisfactory, employees are likely to find different work (J. M. Johnson & Ng, 2015; Kultalahti & Viitala, 2014). When salary increases, then millennials are less likely to terminate employment with their current organization, and they are not likely to leave if the organizations continue to invest into the employee. According to the two-factor theory, millennials are highly sensitive about pay, so if the pay seems comparable to their peers, they are likely to stay (J. M. Johnson & Ng, 2015). Maslow's hierarchy of needs and Herzberg's two-factor theory comprise the motivation aspects for millennials. However, the generational theory includes the ability to understand and explain the differences in each generation.

The equity theory has a few characteristics that are applicable to Herzberg's and to Vroom's theories regarding input. Adams's equity theory relates to how much input a person puts forth versus the outputs the person receives in return for the individual's effort (Adams & Jacobsen, 1964). People possess knowledge of what a fair balance is between inputs and outputs, where fairness motivates individuals (Adams, 1965). Inputs are the individual efforts applied within our work while outputs are the rewards received from that work in return (Armache, 2012). The determination of equality links to the satisfaction of reducing the inequalities within a given situation (Adams & Jacobsen, 1964). The greater an individual's perception of equity, the more motivated that person will be (Hartmann & Slapničar, 2012). Fairness is a measure of one's own belief about the input versus output and how they align with the regards to the ratio of input versus output (Armache, 2012). Millennial leaders who feel others are receiving different treatment or have more resources available are likely to feel more dissatisfied with the outcome.

Regardless of the inequality that millennial leaders experience, they have the ability to change that inequality. The inequality they feel is a negative tension they can release by (a) changing input (not so much effort), (b) determining a different partner to compare outcomes, (c) changing their outcome, (d) changing their self-perception, (e) changing their perception of others, or (f) quitting their job (Adams, 1965). By reducing the negative tension of the inequality experienced, a person feels motivated to do something to alleviate tension through the above actions.

A need exists to understand the differences between input and output within the equity theory. Inputs for work involvement include loyalty, hard work, ability, skill, commitment, trustworthy leadership, and enthusiasm (Adams & Jacobsen, 1964). Rewards are what millennial leaders gain from their output and include financial gains such as pay, benefits, and pension. Nonfinancial gains from outputs consist of recognition, travel, achievement, and promotional opportunities (Hartmann & Slapničar, 2012). According to the equity theory, the outputs of work conditions and pay are not enough to determine motivation. The comparison of ratios for others who experience the same input and similar outputs ultimately determines motivation (Hartmann & Slapničar, 2012). The balance of the ratio of inputs and outputs is important to the motivation experienced through financial and nonfinancial gains.

Millennial leaders, as well aspiring individuals, want to see their efforts rewarded. The basis of expectancy theory is the premise that a person believes that exerting a given amount of effort will lead to high performance (Blotnicky, Mann, & Joy, 2015; Hema Malini & Washington, 2014; Vroom, 1964). The central theme of expectancy theory is the level of attainment of the outcome defines the behavior of an individual (Ramli & Jusoh, 2015). The concept of expectancy is dependent not only on the choices that individuals make, but also on the events beyond their control

(Vroom, 1964). Millennial leaders are similar to other individuals who expect rewards when achieving desired results. Executive leaders in organizations that employ millennial leaders will likely need to recognize millennials when their effort is relevant to the accomplishment.

The art of motivation includes various methods on how to support people to accomplish goals and can be subjective in the process. Individuals feel motivated when a goal is attainable and they have a belief they can achieve (Renko, Kroeck, & Bullough, 2012; Vroom, 1964). Expectancy theory encompasses the relationship between an individual's performance and the outcomes of that individual's efforts, which means humans are psychological beings who gain motivation and inspiration through achieving personal goals and organizational objectives (Berson et al., 2015; Vroom, 1964). A person is likely to act in a certain way when the expectation is that effort will lead to the given outcome (Ramli & Jusoh, 2015). Individuals possess the motivation to achieve their goals due to the relationship between the outcome and the individual's performance.

There are two different expectancy levels within the expectancy theory. The expectancy theory encompasses the belief that individuals believe that their efforts will lead to a specific performance (Expectancy 1), which will then lead to a performance worthy of a reward (Expectancy 2; Hayyat, 2012). Expectancy 2 is the understanding that an individual's level of performance creates extrinsic rewards, such as promotion, recognition, security, and pay (Hayyat, 2012). The two expectancy levels merge to include the input characteristics associated with the event, along with the reaction of the outputs.

The components of the expectancy theory include expectancy, instrumentality, and valence. Expectancy consists of the given amount of effort that will lead to the desired performance. Instrumentality refers to an individual receiving a reward based on performance (Lazaroiu, 2015; Renko et al., 2012). Valence is the actual value an individual places on the reward (Renko et al., 2012; Vroom, 1964). An example of valence is a reward that has to be attractive for someone to want or that person may feel unmotivated or unsatisfied.

Millennial leaders need to feel appreciated for their efforts,which could include, but may not be limited to, pay, promotion, and job security. These individuals also want their employers to understand their psychological well-being through communicating how the members of the organization value their input and career goals. The expectancy theory refers to many variables of managing millennial leaders by establishing the relationship between effort, performance, rewards, and personal goals (Parijat & Bagga, 2014). Millennial leaders are likely to understand that the inputs or actionable steps toward the desired rewards will translate into the expected results.

The extensive information provided about Maslows is imperative to a deep understanding of motivation. The information in this section provided a good foundation for a deeper understanding about motivation and how it has affected the millennials' decision making. Understanding the decision making will help in being able to provide the necessary to tools to save the knowledge of these core leaders.

6 WORKFORCE

The current workplace includes one of the most diverse populations, and for the first time, four generational cohorts are working together. Generational differences did not receive recognition until baby boomers and members of Generation X started working together, which led to the emergence of new research. A group of individuals who share experiences and birth years comprises a generation cohort (Kowske, Rasch, & Wiley, 2010). Economic, political, or cultural texts that evolve and the historical events that shape values influence individuals in each generation (Soulez & Soulez, 2014). Members in each generation proceed through a time that includes critical factors that influence their generation (M. Brown, 2012). Specifically, the need for research emerged from the differences in behaviors, attitudes, habits, and expectations of each generation in the workplace (Young, Sturts, Ross, & Kim, 2013). Each generational cohort possesses values that emerged from the traditions passed down from previous generations.

Each generation has a distinct perspective on employment based on the innate characteristics for that generation. These generational views can include challenges for employers of each generation and how they support the generation cohorts currently in the workforce (Kapoor &

Solomon, 2011). Multigenerational symbiosis is a major topic of interest due to longer life expectancies and to delays in retirement due to economic hardships (Zopiatis et al., 2012). Each generation is a particular length of time that usually includes 20 to 25 years (Zopiatis et al., 2012). There is a long history of different generations and the experiences that made each generation unique, as described by Strauss and Howe.

Comprehending the attributes of generational differences is essential to recognize how researchers should proceed in their research. The approach for developing generations is worthy to note for this research because of the emergence of new generations and older generations coupled with historic social change (Kowske et al., 2010). Strauss and Howe, who are pioneers in generational theory, published the book *Generations: The History of America's Future 1584 to 2069*, which many researchers consider the baseline for generational theory.

Researchers have employed generational theory to distinguish four different generations that are currently working together in the workforce. The generation groups consist baby boomers (1946-1964); Generation X (1965-1979); and the millennials (1980-2000; Schullery, 2013). According to Acar (2014), the term generation means groups that are recognizable based on their age, location, birth, and important events that make individuals who they are. Millennials are better prepared than previous generation in the workforce due to the evolution of systematic changes from one generation to the next.

Life experiences influence individuals' value system and shape personalities that help them identify what is right and wrong. The definition of generation includes individual attributes that share common situations, habits, and culture (Acar, 2014; Zopiatis et al., 2012). Only 22% of millennials believe their peers are ethical, whereas 58% believe that their own cohort is ethical (VanMeter, Grisaffe, Chonko, & Roberts, 2013).

Generation Y members are skeptical about the other generational cohorts, as well as their own. As each generation is different from the previous one, it is interesting to see how some generations seem to have many of the same comparisons. Generational differences are a point of emphasis due to the emergence of the different characteristics discussed previously that need addressing to achieve harmony among employees and leadership.

To increase organizational effectiveness and leadership, managers need to be able to identify generational differences. Growing up during a given period helped popularize the notion that individuals in a specific time of life tend to share similar attitudes, behavior, values, and beliefs (Costanza, Badger, Fraser, Severt, & Gade, 2012). According to Costanza et al. (2012), age exemplifies the variations between individuals associated with particular groups caused by maturation, current life span, and other age-related components. Other factors include events that transpired during the life cycle of each generation that affected attitudes and shaped behaviors, such as World War II, the Great Depression, the civil rights movement, and the terrorist attacks that occurred on September 11, 2001 (Costanza et al., 2012). Strauss and Howe described 18 generations since 1585, which included the baby boom (16th), Generation X (17th), and Generation Y (18th).

Mannheim (1952) noted the basis of sociological phenomena is the biological tempo of birth and death within a generation. Mannheim also noted that individuals belong to the same generation or age group with which they share a common place in social and historical movements. This process predisposes a generation to a characteristic mode of experience and thought (Mannheim, 1952). Generational theory initially seemed like an insignificant revelation but became popular among researchers because of its effects on harmony and productivity in the workplace.

There is significant interest in the generation theory concept because of the need to manage individuals from different generations. According to Saba (2013), the results of studies have not supported the generational theory concept. Researchers have raised questions about the empirical evidence that supports differences in the generation theory, along with the methodological challenges associated with studying them (Costanza et al., 2012). Despite the disagreements, there is enough interest and documentation to justify the need for additional studies and the importance of generational theory. The theory is popular because of the four distinct generation cohorts in the workforce and because millennials are seemingly the most difficult generation to manage.

Theoretical frameworks have not supported the existence of systematic differences between the expectations regarding working conditions, generational values, attitudes, and behavior about work. The basis of the differences in needs, values, and beliefs could be opinions and shaky findings (Saba, 2013). Well-known articles have included claims on how generational differences affect specific occupational outcomes such as risk-taking, satisfaction, commitment, motivation, and leadership style (Costanza et al., 2012). The difference with the general findings of the generation cohorts may become more apparent as employees work into their later years.

As employees are working later in life, and may leave jobs to take advantage of bigger opportunities, organizational leaders need to attract and retain talent more than ever. Millennials require proper working conditions that lead to positive behaviors and retention in the workforce (Campione, 2014; Gilbert, 2011; Saba, 2013). Due to the current and long-term economic situation, baby boomers may continue working into their golden years.

How a group generation cooperates in a situation and the events that ensue help define each generation. It is important to note that these events that occur during certain generations define that generation. Mannheim's (1952) revelations about the social phenomenon of generations represented a certain category for generation location. Mannheim was precise about each group's economic and social conditions. Generation location comprises certain patterns of thought and experiences brought into existence by data from one generation to the next (Mannheim, 1952). Generational differences in the past created an us-versus-them mentality and a need to overcome differences where coworkers affect the relationship significantly (Kralj, Kandampully, & Sonet, 2012). The objectives of the generation cohorts determine these generational differences.

Research about a new generation originates with an instinct that a new generation has developed, which occurs in view of historical settings that include macro changes that affect institutions and individuals. Mannheim (1952) noted that political, economic, and sociocultural orientations distinguish new generations from new cohorts. The use of the word *generation* to denote a cohort refers to individuals proceeding through age groups, where the younger workers replace older workers in the workplace, and everyday events influence the changes that occur (Festing & Schafer, 2014; Kulik, Ryan, Harper, & George, 2014). Ultimately, this is where the pendulum swings from an older generation to the next generation. As individuals identify with generations, organizational leaders and experts help determine specific trends in developing future generations.

Specific progressions take place before a new generation receives recognition. Certain changes need to transpire, and then those experts for identifying generations must detail these macro changes before applying them to research and denoting a generation. For example, the macro changes include the cultural revolution of the 1960s and early 1970s, the economic recession of the late 1970s and early 1980s, and World War II.

These events noted above were all dynamic influencer for the respective generation. Therefore, a generation must accommodate three criteria: (a) behavior of individuals in cohorts will identify with the effects on generations during their formative years and then 10 years after, (b) explanations of the behavior of people in groups must demonstrate differences when comparing generations, and (c) generations need to show a form of institutionalization (Parry & Urwin, 2011). It can be difficult to locate the exact beginning and end of a generation date, and many theorists have slight differences according to the appropriate beginning and ending of generation time periods.

Every birth cohort experiences a different youth and childhood compared to its predecessors, but this does not make every new cohort a new generation. Historical events have distinguished different generations since 1584 (Roberts, 2012). With each generational cohort having a variety of experiences, occupational beliefs, and values, scholars try to determine the similarities and differences (Parry & Urwin, 2011). A multitude of factors ranging from life events to significant changes in lifestyle are attributed to differences in the generational gap.

Life experiences are the parts of each generation that have been influential in society and the workforce and comprise key attitudes and behaviors of specific members. According to Shragay and Tziner (2011), the *generational effect* is a phenomenon where information is gathered with regards to life experiences by contributing to a historical aspect of time during the time they have lived. Not everyone agreed that the term generational effect is appropriate due to overlapping of the age groups. The overlaps in age are a common issue that has plagued studies of various sociology measurements and generational theory as a whole.

As researchers continue to explore the overlapping age phenomenon, they should replicate studies to show a comparable amount of research for the significance of the generation effect and the ways leaders can better motivate and manage the different levels of personalities. Additional studies are likely to demonstrate the impact of new knowledge in the field. These studies may include the newest generation, known as Generation Z. Researchers will likely have an interest in the commonalities of Generation Z and their relationships to past generations.

The gap in the generational shift consists of leadership responsibility and the impact on employment in each generation cohort. Kralj et al. (2012) reviewed the differences in work values from generation to generation and discussed the importance of understanding generational shifts. With the retirements of baby boomers, and one third of the baby boom employees expected to exit the workforce between 2015 and 2025, their replacements will be Generation X members and millennials (M. Y. Lacey & Groves, 2014). Researchers have accused members of Generation X and millennials of having a weaker work ethic than baby boomers and traditionalists (Moore, Grunberg, & Krause, 2014). The evolving research indicates members of Generation X and millennials value their time off and their social life, which likely means they are less willing to put in long days to finish projects. The literature on generational differences is diverse and requires careful consideration because of the potential risk for survey bias. Baby boomers were influential in the workforce, as they felt dedicated to the organization and their work duties.

The baby boom generation started in Western Europe and North America in the mid-1940s. Baby boomers claimed it was more important to position the company first than to put their individualistic needs first (Kapoor & Solomon, 2011). Baby boomers also put work ahead of family as their identity was attached to work versus attached to family. This was an important characteristic trait noted by Gen X because this would separate many families, which is why Gen X was characterized as the 'latchkey' children. This generation was successful in the workplace. However, it was also associated with divorces and broken families.

Baby boomers are the first generation in human history to reach significant wealth compared to past generations, as they earned more at every age compared to previous generations (Chand & Tung, 2014). The baby boomers experienced significant changes in culture and in the workforce. The term baby boom refers to the growth in the birthrate for newborns when troops returned home after World War II (Gentry, Griggs, Deal, Mondore, & Cox, 2011). The group was a privileged cohort because its members grew up in a healthy economy (Roberts, 2012). The labor markets were full of employment opportunities, as middle-class jobs increased significantly in the early years (Roberts, 2012). The baby boomers were respectful of authority and felt that hard work was the way to succeed in life.

Baby boomers established a foundation of success through perseverance and hard work by being part of a population of 80 million. The members of this generation worked long hours and did not spend time with the family as a result (Schoch, 2012). The millennials and members of Generation X acknowledged baby boomers worked hard only to be let go or laid off during difficult economic periods (Roberts, 2012). Baby boomers' long work hours led to members of the following generations valuing time off.

Advancing human knowledge changed from a simplistic lifestyle to a more advanced lifestyle with the addition of household necessities that were not common prior to the 1950s. The baby boomers were the beneficiaries of increased living standards that included car and home ownership, foreign travel, television, computers, and Internet technologies (Roberts, 2012). Common characteristics of baby boomers include being materialistic and feeling stressed to achieve their goals, along with their financial status (Costanza et al., 2012). The advent of television shaped baby boomers. In 1950, only 12% of households had a television, but by 1958, 83% had at least one (Schullery, 2013). The baby boomers experienced extreme changes in technology and the ability to travel and developed an appetite for what life has to offer.

The baby boomers grew up in the 1950s and 1960s. As they were the largest generation in history until the millennials, and they had to be competitive due to so many people vying for the same positions. There is a consensus that baby boomers are known for the following: workaholics, self-motivated, self-centered, and not appreciative of what they accomplished (Coulter & Faulkner, 2014; Verschoor, 2013). Baby boomers want it all and were willing to grow and change as needed to expand their talents, which meant working long hours and being ruthless to obtain success, including material success.

Baby boomers do not like change, and were likely to be complacent with the way they conducted business. Baby boomers typically prefer hands-on experiences and are detailed oriented (Dimitriou & Blum, 2015). Baby boomers are the last generation that thought it was a good idea to stay with the same organization for an entire career (Schullery, 2013). While baby boomers continued to show a high work ethic within their jobs, families began to change and divorce rates increased. Higher divorce rates led to members of Generation X becoming latchkey kids in the 1980s and 1990s.

Baby boomers were the last generation that grew up with two full-time working parents. However, baby boomers began to experience single-parent households as divorces became more common. The baby boomers experienced a significant amount of social change during their youth, so they learned to embrace growth and change (Gibson et al., 2011). Baby boomers have had to work longer than expected because, as of 2014, almost 60% of the labor pool over age 55 had amassed less than $100,000 for retirement, while 24% had secured less than $1,000. Two thirds of baby boomers did not plan to retire or planned to work past age 65 (Irving, 2015). Baby boomers not retiring is a concern that also prevents members of Generation X from opportunities for advancements. The inability to withdraw from the workforce will affect both generations negatively. Generation X is the smallest generation when compared to the baby boomers and the millennials.

Members of Generation X grew up in a volatile environment due to the large number of single-parent households and having to defend themselves, which influenced their actions in the workplace. Many Generation X members were latchkey children, as they were the first generation to have parents living separately (Gibson et al., 2011). Generation X is also the smallest generation in terms of the population and represented only 27% of the adult population in 2014 (Pew Research Center, 2014). Common characteristics among members of Generation X are loyalty, independence, being a slouch, and feeling inspired primarily by monetary rewards in the workplace. Generation X was also the first generation whose members believed in having fun in the workplace (Gibson et al., 2011; Young et al., 2013). Members of Generation X began to have fun because they saw their parents having only serious attitudes while sacrificing their family for work.

Generation X members value a good work–life balance that enables them to enjoy nonwork activities. Members of Generation X value a good work–life balance because many of their parents were let go from organizations after years of service (Kapoor & Solomon, 2011). Generation X members are the children of workaholic baby boomers and saw their parents spend their lives with one organization (Tang, Cunningham, Frauman, & Perry, 2012). Members of Generation X also experienced a high parental divorce rate and lived in single-parent homes (Thomas, 2011).

Members of this group are self-sufficient in many ways because they had to fend for themselves. Growing up as latchkey adolescents is one of the main reasons that Generation X members have become such a large part of their millennial children's lives, as they did not receive a lot of support growing up. The differences between baby boomers and Generation X members is that Generation X members live to work while baby boomers work to live (Lai, Chang, & Hsu, 2012). The significant differences between baby boomers and members of Generation X can strain relationships between the generations.

Members of Generation X spent their early years in daycare and their later years being at home alone in single-parent households, so the focus for this cohort was to value freedom and individualism. Generation X members are not willing to overwork at the expense of sacrificing quality of life; therefore, they prefer a good balance (Lai et al., 2012). Members of Generation X do not want to allow work to be their only focus. Generation X members have a strong opinion on their work ethic and on how they view their leisure time, and they are not willing to sacrifice their free time.

Members of Generation X grew up with a significant amount of autonomy, as it was common to be at home alone at an early age. Not having the proper supervision during key adolescent years caused some problems. Members of Generation X are also self-disciplinarians, as they had to decide to do homework rather than watch cable television while their working parents were away (Schoch, 2012). Besides the influence of the separation of their parents during their growth years, members of Generation X also endured world crisis. Global competition, AIDS, and new technological advancements occurred during their growth years.

Generation X was the first generation actively involved in technological advancements that included having an Internet provider and being able to surf the web, which became a revolutionary part of society.

Members of Generation X value life options, flexibility, and the ability to balance work (O'Bannon, 2001). Generation X members are also loyal to their career, skills, and themselves (Lai et al., 2012). Similar to Generation Y members, members of Generation X lost their faith in work institutions as they saw their parents laid off or terminated after investing their life in one company (Marston, 2007). Generation X members have some common themes that are important to baby boomers and millennials, who are team driven, but Generation X members became independent and self-sufficient because of their lack of parental supervision during their growth years.

The retirement of baby boomers will create further opportunities for Generation X members and millennials. Baby boomers embracing their jobs for such a long period minimized the amount of executive leadership responsibility available for Generation X members and affects millennials' career progression. After waiting decades because baby boomers held onto their senior leadership roles for an extended time, members of Generation X will be in charge of key leadership positions around 2019 (Schultz & Schwepker, 2012). There will be significant changes due to the workforce they will be leading, which will include millennials who need different managing styles to ensure success.

One significant change will be a more collaborative decision-making process that will involve teams around the world. Generation X employees will be in a precarious position when they take on the top leadership positions because they will be taking care of the elderly (baby boomers) while managing a workforce they may have difficulty managing, which includes millennials, due to the different values each group possesses. Open-minded leaders with the ability to satisfy the talent they have on board will be more successful than others (Hong, Hao, Kumar, Ramendran, & Kadiresan, 2012). Strategic awareness encompasses using new methods that include millennials in the decision-making process. The new methods are likely to make a significant difference in satisfying the needs of talented employees through job satisfaction.

7 SATISFACTION

Job satisfaction is an important step for Gen Y leaders and how they feel about their overall work. Research includes key indicators such as job satisfaction, which is instrumental in the success of individuals being happy within their current workplace, which helps elevate employee retention. Herzberg noted the importance of satisfaction and dissatisfaction among employees and the ways they affect employee morale (Hofmans, Gieter, & Pepermans, 2013). I will discuss the dynamics of how satisfaction acts as a predictor of why an individual is likely to continue with the same job for a greater length of time compared to the results of job dissatisfaction.

The discussion of job satisfaction was important at the turn of the 20th century. In 1919, Eberle mentioned job satisfaction when discussing a person capable of performing a particular job but not content to do so due to the specific activity or work environment. According to Eberle, it was common for the job to become more satisfactory, and baby boomers would stay with the same company until they permanently left the workforce. However, millennials and members of Generation X witnessed layoffs and the mistreatment of baby boomers who dedicated their life to their company.

Having more choices over a career may increase the level of happiness and satisfaction toward work. Individual workers who have increased volition and fewer constraints are likely to have higher work-related well-being (Duffy, Autin, & Bott, 2015). Work volition is likely to play a vital role in life satisfaction and employee retention, which is a measurement of a subjective experience of freedom to make career choices from an individual's sense of self-conception (Vroom, 1964). Employees leaving an organization sacrifice a perceived level of material and psychological benefits (Kraimer, Shaffer, Harrison, & Ren, 2012). The negative correlation between career barriers and work volition refers to job dissatisfaction (Duffy et al., 2015). The more volition an individual accumulates, the more likely that individual will experience success and retention in the workplace. The ability to ensure success in a person's career is likely to be an indicator of how an individual performs on the job.

Job satisfaction can signify different outcomes for different individuals or have a variety of meanings for different generations. Therefore, satisfaction for baby boomers can vary from job satisfaction for millennials because of their disparate backgrounds. For example, baby boomers entered the workforce around 1963, and computer technology was not common within the corporate foundation because baby boomers did not believe technology would be an integral part of society. However, millennials grew up in the age of computer technology and are more likely adaptable to rapid technological changes (Elias, Smith, & Barney, 2012). Job satisfaction for baby boomers may be the importance of doing a job well regardless of how many hours they need to spend.

Work imbalance for millennials can be a cause for lower job satisfaction. M. Brown (2012) noted that intense working conditions hurt job satisfaction. There are notable differences in the perceptions of a work balance between millennials and baby boomers. Millennials' perception of work balance includes hours worked, the work intensification involved, and the negative reaction toward work balance.

In addition to the external elements associated with job satisfaction, there are internal aspects regarding personalities and attitudes that can either skew or promote job satisfaction. Self-esteem has a positive correlation to job satisfaction. Identity theory can help clarify how a transition at work can alter or enhance an individual's self-esteem (Kraimer et al., 2012). Self-esteem can predict changes in job satisfaction (Orth, Robins, & Widaman, 2012). Job satisfaction increases as individuals age, because individuals can better match their skill level with the right job as they mature in the job market.

The staff at *Fortune* magazine ranked Google the best company to work for in the United States in 2012. A noteworthy reason is that Google engineers receive a minimum of 1 day per week to work on whatever project they would like, which encourages employees to solve problems, explore new ideas, and learn new skills (McIntyre, Mattingly, Lewandowski, & Simpson, 2014). This type of job satisfaction is congruent with research that shows individuals with self-expanding collaboration within their organization experience self-growth that will lead to greater job satisfaction and commitment (McIntyre et al., 2014). Job satisfaction is comparable with longevity in the workplace, especially when the opportunity for self-growth is available.

Individuals in workplaces that include self-expansion have unique, challenging tasks and should experience a higher degree of self-growth that leads to increased job satisfaction. A career is a big part of the make-up of an individual, along with whether the workplace consists of opportunities for self-expansion versus having a mundane work environment (Kraimer et al., 2012). I have observed a parallel between organizations whose leaders demonstrate commitment to employee growth through creativity versus assigning tasks to complete. Companies appear to have a renewed commitment to identifying methods to increase retention by finding ways to improve job satisfaction.

Individuals who have a proper understanding of employee motivation can secure relationships within the workforce. Employee motivation first appeared in the 4th century B.C., when hedonism was a driving force for behavior (Korzynski, 2013). Motivation alludes to the inner motivation coming from within a person with characteristics such as intensity, persistence, and proper direction to achieve explicit goals that are not due to natural ability (Purohit & Bandyopadhyay, 2014). According to Vroom (1964), the further motivated individuals are, the more likely their performance is to improve. Work is a psychological process that maintains, energizes, and directs action toward a particular work function (Purohit & Bandyopadhyay, 2014). Elias et al. (2012) noted, "Work motivation is a set of energetic forces that originate both within as well as beyond an individual's being, to initiate work-related behavior, and to determine its form, direction, intensity, and duration" (p. 456). Individuals have different trigger points that assist in determining level of motivation. Motivational tools will be successful if a person is willing to listen.

Understanding human motivation has been a formidable problem for centuries, as some of the most influential thinkers, such as Adam Smith, Aristotle, Abraham Maslow, and Sigmund Freud, have struggled to understand it (Nohria, Groysberg, & Lee, 2008). In the early 1900s, Frederick Taylor founded scientific management, which played a role in the experimental process of breaking down simple tasks to enhance productivity (Nohria et al., 2008). The idea behind scientific management was to motivate employees by establishing simpler tasks that would generate work motivation. The system of motivation involves a connection between rewarding employees and production achieved, which includes a subjective evaluation of the employee by measuring the productivity evaluation of the performance reward (Muscalu & Muntean, 2013). However, further research demonstrated a disconnection exists between early work motivation literature and later knowledge.

Mayo managed the experimental process at the Hawthorne plant of the Western Electric Company. The reason for the experiment was to observe the lighting and its effect on employee productivity. The results of the research were perplexing because production went up in the experimental room as well as the control room when the lighting increased. The Hawthorne experiment was notable as being a part of the most remarkable paradigm shift in history due to the relationship with scientific management and human relations. The opposite also occurred: when the lighting decreased, the production of the employees still increased (Hassard, 2012). The researchers concluded that the increased attention toward the workers at the Hawthorne plant affected workers' progress, regardless of the elements.

Mayo understood that two concerns occurred during the initial experiment: the experimenter effect and the social effect. The experimenter effect was a perception that management cared about the employees by making changes to enhance the employees' well-being (Hassard, 2012). The outcome of the Hawthorne study was the Hawthorne effect, which indicated that social relations, not the physical environment, shaped organizational outcomes while influencing the social relations movement in the workforce (Zhong & House, 2012). The social effect developed due to separation from others that allowed individuals to advance camaraderie among peers to improve work performance. The Hawthorne effect was responsible for ushering in human relations among employees, which was a significant breakthrough because the employees at the Hawthorne plant worked together and felt the bosses were looking after their interests.

Over time with psychological and management ideology, many job enrichment programs have added to the value of employee motivation or had an adverse effect. Human resource personnel have embraced and adopted philosophies targeting and creating learning organizations (Casad, 2012). Ongoing systematic attempts to motivate employees by manipulating the motivation factors have been unsuccessful. When employees become bored or disengaged, something is lacking in their job (Van der Heijden, Schepers, & Nijssen, 2012). One of the best opportunities to improve jobs and make them more appealing is to distribute or add duties to employees to energize them by focusing on their strengths (Levoy, 2014). It is important to provide capable individuals a chance to grow.

Managers have learned through trial and error that they have to manage the Generation Y cohort differently. Tulgan (2013) noted that management needs to plug into the enthusiasm and excitement that millennials bring on the first day of work or they are at risk of turning a good hire into a bad one. This practice will assist in promoting individuals to continue with the same motivation when they were initially hired. It is imperative to turn every demand and request into opportunities to earn performance-based rewards and to go the extra mile (Tulgan, 2013). Outstanding employees operate at peak performance, demonstrate engagement, and possess significant energy levels (Levoy, 2014). Employees who satisfy these elements experience the essence of job enrichment.

The availability of motivational concepts has expanded over the years. Most motivational employee concepts emerged in the 20th century and affected the way leaders manage their employees. Nohria et al. (2008) illustrated a reproduction of employee motivation that included specifics for motivation. The model of employee motivation consists of four components: commitment, satisfaction, engagement, and intention to quit or stay with the organization. The morale of an employee is an imperative criterion associated with motivation that links the employee's perception concerning the job and the organization (Islam & Ali, 2013). To increase motivation, organizational leaders need to satisfy all four drivers by developing an organizational culture to provide best practices for mutual collaboration, sharing, and reliance.

With members of the new millennial generation in key leadership positions, numerous changes are occurring. These changes are materializing because this generation is so different from previous generations. A direct manager is necessary to foster a highly motivating environment by offering recognition, praise, and encouragement of teamwork (Korzynski, 2013). Leaders will need to adjust how they manage and lead the new technological generation. The key to managing is to understand that individuals comprehend the world differently according to their perceptions (Kilber et al., 2014). It is imperative to pay particular attention to the preferred communication requirements to communicate and motivate employees through creative tools to retain them.

The need for employee motivation has increased with millennials entering the workforce. Organizational leaders are paying attention to the managers managing this group because peers see millennials as disloyal, needy, casual, and having a sense of entitlement (Moss & Martins, 2014; C. Thompson & Gregory, 2012). Comprehension is the answer for managers to be able to motivate and retain the millennial workforce through all the challenges that the millennials present. Millennials' commitment and retention relate to a healthy relationship with their immediate managers (C. Thompson & Gregory, 2012). If leaders plan for their companies to flourish in the future, managers will need to implement new leadership and management styles that relate to young employees' work capabilities, beginning with timely feedback.

Emotional intelligence is an aspect of the human persona that enables individuals to make rational decisions. Effective leaders can capitalize on emotional intelligence to motivate others by controlling their emotions and using this power to motivate employees (Sand, Cangemi, & Ingram, 2011). According to a survey in 1996, employees have a different perception of what is important to employees versus what employers believe (Sand et al., 2011). Researchers ranked items between 1 and 10 for importance, where a full appreciation of work was rated first for millennial employees and eighth for management.

Supervisors concluded good wages were the most important criterion for employees, but the employees ranked good wages fifth. Employees rated being sympathetic to understanding personal problems as third, and employers thought employees would rate it ninth (Sand et al., 2011). A disconnect existed between what company leaders viewed as important and what made employees happy. Leaders should understand that money is not a key motivator for individuals to excel in their career. The measurement helped facilitate the notion that generations' perceptions have changed.

Finding common ground to inspire others to fulfill their goals by desiring to accomplish them capitalizes on the power of motivation. Effective leaders and motivators can use these talents to motivate and retain others. Leaders have the responsibility to attain goals for the viability of the organization by meeting or exceeding the competition. The leaders must create a culture that promotes motivation and will help individuals to feel inspired to help accomplish the goals set forth (Sand et al., 2011). Developing a culture will assist in promoting an environment that offers inspiration and motivation.

Creating a harmonious work atmosphere can be more important than compensation through motivation, optimism while hoping to engage millennial employees in exceeding their capabilities. The lack of emotional awareness by a person in leadership can cause unnecessary conflict and be a de-motivator (Sand et al., 2011). Effective leadership is vital to lead an organization through difficult times while motivating others to achieve the objectives needed for success. Leaders are likely to be more successful when they can promote a balanced culture while being able to manage emotions.

There is no shortage of quotations or ideas for motivation. President Dwight D. Eisenhower stated, "Motivation is the art of getting people to do what you want them to do because they want to do it" (Hauser, 2014, p. 246). The concept of motivation is necessary and evokes individuals to carry out a series of activities to appease them (Achim, Dragolea, & Balan, 2013). Tulgan (2009) posited that the self-esteem movement and Generation Y's vulnerability to new ventures have chipped away the motivation for millennials. Generation Y members enjoy being in a safe environment where someone is keeping track of their accomplishments and they enjoy receiving credit for their achievements.

Millennials want to negotiate small rewards that continue to provide them with the motivation to win because they want more of everything. Researchers have noted the greatest motivators are not monetary rewards. However, the perception of achievement, recognition, responsibility, fame, and pleasure from challenges and social interactions are important (Dimitriou & Blum, 2015). Part of employee motivation that Tulgan (2009) discussed is a point system that motivates Generation Y members to finish projects while meeting high-quality standards to receive rewards according to the total points they accrue. Leaders of organizations understand that it requires more resources to motivate the members of Generation Y. Growing up in a different era that consistently promoted positive inspiration to succeed puts organization leaders in a precarious position when reviewing the millennial generation because the members of

Generation Y have rarely experienced loss or faced punishment for their failures.

8 MILLENIAL LEADER RETENTION

We have had the chance to review all the generations, key theorist and motivational concepts, which has provided the foundation for what is important. The question is how do we retain Gen Y leaders? We will begin to peel the onion back even further for a comprehensive understanding. With the business climate continuously changing, and to provide exceptional service and run their business efficiently, organizational leaders must promote internal and external motivation within the work environment. Achieving this goal requires employee appreciation, ongoing communication with employees, high employee morale, proper motivation, feedback from employees, and low employee turnover (Dumitrescu, Cetina, & Pentescu, 2012). Managers have detected generational differences such as salary expectation management techniques, workplace styles, work–life balance, education, and autonomy; the essential aspect for organizational success is accepting the new generation (Kilber et al., 2014). Employers may need to focus on employee retention problems moving forward.

Members of management ought to focus on keeping their top employees if they are fulfilling their requirements. According to a recent benefits study on the forces that affect attitudes, employee benefits, and trends, the feedback received indicated almost half of all the workers surveyed were looking for a new job in 2012 (Tillman, 2013). According to Tillman (2013), the war for talent accelerates when the economy improves, so it becomes increasingly important to retain high-quality employees by understanding why they are leaving the organization. Tillman (2013) demonstrated the need to understand the feedback employees are providing. Business leaders are looking to reduce the dissatisfaction level while increasing the retention rate among employees.

Retaining good employees is difficult, but leaders can take some steps to demonstrate approaches to increase job satisfaction and reduce the negative barriers between employers and employees. Tillman (2013) indicated that the majority of workers who were probably going to depart from their current position described themselves as the kind of worker that company leaders should attempt to retain. The principal reasons that employees were contemplating leaving their current role included (a) they felt their employers were not taking care of them, (b) they felt financially or physically stressed, (c) they felt dissatisfied with their jobs, and (d) they did not believe their company had a good reputation (Oladapo, 2014; Tillman, 2013). After identifying the reason, employers need to make the appropriate changes.

Knowing why employees are looking to leave creates an opportunity to offer assistance or benefits to staying versus leaving. Retention improves when employers provide a supportive work culture; can develop and advance; and offer compensation, benefits, and a work–life balance (Oladapo, 2014). Organization leaders are beginning to understand that there is a war for talent, so they must provide strong incentives to promote employee retention if they are going to stay competitive.

Employee turnover can be an expensive obstacle for many organization leaders. According to Akila (2012), it is important to retain employees by helping them feel valued in the organization. Employee turnover costs organizations over $25 billion each year in the United States due to the cost of hiring and training new employees (McKeown, 2010). It is important to acknowledge that the turnover cost will increase if we do not combat the problem now. This is opportunity to begin advancing human performance by recognizing and minimizing the reasons why millennials leaders leave the organization. Leadership within an organization will likely classify the cost of lost production indirectly or directly as acquisition, learning, or separation costs.

A limited amount of turnover can be healthy for bringing in innovative perspectives. However, scholars view turnover as mostly negative because it is costly to replace individuals and can give the impression an organization is a bad employer (Kellison et al., 2013; D. Liu et al., 2012). It is imperative to locate cost-effective measures to retain good employees within the workforce to save time and money for employers by reducing the number of valued employees leaving their organizations.

Most business-savvy individuals are likely to agree that turnover rates must improve. The problem is many organization leaders fail to recognize a turnover problem (Hartmann & Rutherford, 2015). For those individuals who endured pay cuts, bonus losses, and corporate restructuring during the recent economic turmoil in the United States, organizational leaders must come up with strategic plans so employees do not continue to leave their positions (McKeown, 2010). A relationship exists between employee retention and a benefit to the organization that includes the following (Akila, 2012):

1. Loss of company knowledge: Employee takes valuable knowledge about the organization when leaving.

2. Interruption of customer service: This includes the potential loss of clients due to the relationships developed with the employee.

3. Turnover leads to more turnover: There is a negative feeling among the remaining employees when employees terminate their employment.

4. Goodwill of the company: Strong retention rates encourage potential employees to join organizations because it shows organizational consistency.

5. Regaining efficiency: Due to the loss of knowledge in a department, employees increase the time spent training a new employee.

It is easy to identify why employees leave their organizations, but it is a challenge to find ways to improve retention. According to Tillman (2013), offering programs that help with work–life balance, continuing education, psychological assistance, debt management, and benefits options to protect families can help improve retention. Tillman discovered that employees who felt satisfied or extremely satisfied were six times more likely to stay than those who felt dissatisfied with benefits.

It is crucial when companies have benefits packages that leaders communicate the value of that package. A comprehensive benefits package can have a significant effect on retaining employees (Tillman, 2013). According to Oladapo (2014), poor hiring practices increase turnover because current staff can feel disappointed with the revolving door of employees due to the time and demand new employees put on them. New employees mismatched for a job will exit an organization quickly when there is no alignment. This is an ongoing issue that has business leaders perplexed because most organizations have extensive hiring and onboarding procedures. In many cases, there may not be a mismatched job, as it is more about a culture dump. Meaning, the culture is likely toxic and the millennial leader desires no part.

There was less concern about retaining baby boomers as employees because many in this generation would stay with one organization their whole career. Organization leaders have had a difficult time retaining millennials; specifically, managers have found it difficult to manage younger people. Millennials acknowledge the world in their own way compared to previous generations, so the processes used to handle them must be different (Holm, 2012). Trefalt (2013) conducted an in-depth study of how employees bargain between work and nonwork, known as boundary work. Organization leaders and managers who set aside their biases about the millennial generation will have greater success attracting and retaining members of this generation (C. Thompson & Gregory, 2012). The millennials could be the most entrepreneurial generation in the United States, which could cause challenges (Ferri-Reed, 2014a). If this is the case, concern among organization leaders will increase in the future.

If employees experience satisfaction with their current employer, they are likely to recognize leaving as riskier. Holt et al.'s (2012) study about what drives job satisfaction included the following placed in order of importance: (a) challenge, (b) personal growth, (c) and making a positive impact. Holt et al. also demonstrated that the driving force behind millennials is the support of their parents. The strong parental support is no surprise, as millennials' parents sheltered them during their early years.

If a high number of millennials leave the corporate workforce to manage their own companies, organizational leaders will find it challenging to locate additional talent. According to a study of approximately 6,500 managers across six different organizations, the most significant engagement stimulus was the relationships with immediate supervisors who are responsible for managing career development and performance (Gilbert, 2011). Leaders within organizations must create an environment in which millennials can provide resources back to the community to satisfy their generosity and their goal of giving back. It is also noted that employees do not typically leave the company, but they leave their immediate supervisor. Millennial leaders did not value the relationship because their supervisor did not provide feedback, increased opportunity or demonstrate that they are valued by the organization.

Retention and engagement are greater for individuals involved in corporate responsibility programs. According to Moritz (2014), Pricewaterhouse Coopers leadership has increased retention with those involved in corporate responsibility programs by over 1 year; many employees move on to large firms or receive promotions to higher positions. Pricewaterhouse Coopers leaders have been able to work with their management team to help modify the opinions of the millennial cohort by engaging in teamwork, allowing for flexible scheduling, and encouraging education to understand the needs of the millennials. The flexibility and adaptability of leadership personnel have helped extend opportunities for millennial employees through corporate responsibility.

Members of Generation X and baby boomers who struggle to understand millennials because of misconceptions of entitlement and behavior could learn through continuous education. Communication standards will be necessary, as millennials must be able to communicate successfully across multiple generations and multiple cultures (Hartman & McCambridge, 2011). Attempts to retain the millennial cohort will incorporate the ideas of teamwork, corporate responsibility, and understanding a new generation while accommodating their thought processes.

This qualitative research included individual interviews to investigate millennial leadership and ways to retain and motivate this group. The ability to motivate and retain millennials leaders is crucial to the success of corporate America as many baby boomers retire. The generational differences in the workplace are causing managers to act and think differently due to the culture change from previous generations to the millennial cohort. Millennials have different work values and work ethics highlighted through unprecedented corporate responsibility and work–life balance. My expectation was to offer information about the specificities of retention, motivation, and job satisfaction and about the theoretical concepts that would help in moving forward with the interviews. The ability to generate improvements for retention and motivation while ensuring job satisfaction for millennial leadership helped to determine how to retain them within their current organizations.

9 DESIGN

This chapter encapsulates the research design and the approach to the study and the justification of each. The research indicated what was important to millennial leadership and what is needed from the organization to reduce attrition. The discussions entail a brief summary of the problem statement, sample size, sampling method, eligibility criteria, and characteristics of the sample. I collected data using interviews from a sample of millennial leaders who oversaw five or more employees in the service industry in the southwestern United States.

The overarching problem is the high rate of current and projected attrition among Generation Y leaders. The aging workforce and the retirement of baby boomers need addressing, which means executive leaders need to attract and retain members of younger generations because it is not easy to replace or recover lost knowledge (Hokanson et al., 2011). The specific problem addressed in this study is a lack of knowledge and understanding as captured in the scholarly research regarding how the motivation of Generation Y leaders affects employee satisfaction while increasing employee retention factors (Luscombe et al., 2013). The basis of the study converged on this problem of retaining millennial leaders through motivating and satisfying them.

The purpose of this qualitative study was to investigate the effect of motivation on the perceived level of satisfaction and retention for Generation Y cohort leaders within the southwestern United States. More specifically, the study involved determining if Maslow's hierarchy of needs, Vroom's expectancy theory, Adams's equity theory, or Herzberg's two-factor theory affect the lived experiences of Generation Y leaders. The qualitative study helps further the research of millennial leaders and includes a better understanding about how business leaders might employ motivation strategies to increase the satisfaction of Generation Y leaders and therefore decrease their attrition.

This section includes the questions used in this qualitative study and for developing the interview questions. The approach was suitable for this study because the purpose of this approach was to emphasize the lived experiences of the participants. I used three questions to guide my research based on millennial leaders who oversee five or more employees in the service sector within the southwestern United States. Please note the questions were noted earlier in the preceding chapters:

Research Question 1: What are Generation Y leaders' lived experiences and reactions when the leaders of service organizations try to motivate the teams to which they belong in the southwestern United States?

Research Question 2: What factors are causing Generation Y leaders to leave service organizations?

Research Question 3: What role does employer motivation play in the retention of Generation Y leaders in the service industry?

The qualitative methodology was suitable for exploring millennial leadership experiences and perspectives. The exploration included how motivation influences the participants' experiences and perspectives and leads to employee satisfaction and increased retention in the workplace. Selecting subjects for a qualitative research involves ensuring potential participants have the experience the researcher desires through purposive sampling. Researchers cannot evaluate the results of a purposive sample by using a random sampling method (Englander, 2012).

The first task is to find and select participants who have specific and meaningful experiences of a phenomenon (Yuksel & Yildirim, 2015). The desired population for this research was millennial leaders. I selected individuals who met the criteria for overseeing a minimum of five employees, living in the southwestern United States, and working in the service industry while being available and willing to answer questions openly and honestly. The following sections include a brief description of the components of the methodologies chosen: sampling techniques, the setting and sample size, saturation, instrumentation, and field test.

The sampling strategy for my research yielded Generation Y leaders born between 1980 and 1995. These years satisfied a consistent sampling design for a study conducted in 2016, so those who met the criteria were at least 21 years of age. The sample size of 20 participants was suitable because I suspected that I would reach saturation by identifying common themes. Guetterman (2015) posited that some researchers asserted the sample size can depend on the research questions, data collection, data analysis, and availability of resources. Sampling is not just a matter of determining a number, but a matter of reaching information richness (Guetterman, 2015). The determination for the appropriate sample size is contingent on many elements, which means a researcher must find rich information while attempting to reach participant saturation.

Based on the responses, I suggest how individuals who employ Generation Y leaders through a variety of opportunities could satisfy and retain Generation Y leaders through direct or indirect motivation. The first part of the chapter includes the purpose statement and a description of the implementation of the research.

The research setting chosen was the southwestern region of the United States that included California, New Mexico, Arizona, Texas, Colorado, Utah, and Nevada. The study included individuals who worked in the service industry within these states and had at least five individuals under their purview. At the time of the study, the region that I researched consisted of a diversified group of people living and working in the states mentioned above. Due to the broad scope of the participants, I was able to capture the participants' experiences throughout the semistructured interviews.

I attempted to connect with approximately 9,000 people to join my LinkedIn network, with nearly 5,000 accepting my connection invite, which provided more opportunities for them to view my post looking for millennial leaders who met the criteria. Step 3 included joining LinkedIn groups that included millennial leaders, in which I posted invitations to be a candidate if they met the criteria. I generated all 20 individuals via networking through the LinkedIn post. I also shared my LinkedIn posts on Facebook and asked others to share the posts to identify potential candidates.

10 RESULTS

I analyzed the participants' responses and generated seven themes from all the interview data that are the basis for retaining and motivating millennial leaders. These were the common responses among all participants on how they view their career and organization objectives:

1. Work and Life Balance Are Important
2. Recognition of Work Can Be Helpful
3. Welcome High Level of Responsibility
4. Lack of Future Growth
5. Disconnect in Generation Gap
6. The Aspect of Work is Important
7. Importance of Achievement

These seven themes identified areas that many of the participants agreed were important to them. The themes below were noted because of how often each was noted during the interviews. These are themes that every organization leader should take note of and determine what steps are needed to improve each attribute while improving the retention and motivation of the Generation Y leaders. The information below is unique to other books because it provides the conveyed by the participants in their own words. This in return helps us understand how each participant views motivation and retention, along with the perception from other generations.

1. **Work and Life Balance Are Important**

Participants were cognizant of their work and life balance and were confident that they had a work–life balance or they were working to achieve one. The responses about work and life balance demonstrated the desire and importance to reach that balance if the participant did not currently have it or continual attempts to achieve balance. Participant 3 stated,

> You know in the past I have definitely buried myself in my work. I have also definitely been negligent at worst sometimes. I have worked for the same company for 5 years and that happens. There have been ups and downs. But right now, I would have to say I have an excellent work and life balance. I show up for work on time; I work for eight hours.

Participant 17 stated,

> I tend to get more wrapped around in working so much that my social life kind of falls off, but somehow I'm still able to keep a good balance between friends and family, but still able to work at the same time.

Participant 12 asserted,

> That is something that I have struggled with regularly, and I have struggled with that for years. I do kind of let work get the best of me, even outside of the hours of work. That is something that I'm still learning to try to fix, organize, or whatever. It's hard because of course, you need to work. You need to work to survive; priority, and I personally feel like I need to learn to make that my number two priority; my second priority again is my personal or my home life. It's just a job, but it's yours.

Some participants were specific about the importance of work and life balance, along with how it was instrumental for them to stay with their current organization. For example, Participant 6 acknowledged, "This is the one thing that does keep me at this company." Participant 2 stated,

> I'd say this is the best job I've ever had. I work 4 days a week. Next month, I'll be working 1 day from home, and I will be required to go work 3 days a week. So work–family balance; this is the best I've ever seen.

Some participants that felt they achieved work balance seemed to feel less sure about balance as a whole due to concerns about the lack of balance in their personal or home life. Participant 10 stated the following with regard to work–life balance: "I would say I do. I really can't give too much of insight on that just because I have school as well." The participants all agreed that work and life were important and an integral part of their life.

2. Recognition of Work Can Be Helpful

Participants indicated the importance of recognition and of how they were recognized. They identified the different types of recognition that included verbal, public recognition, monetary awards, certificates, client recognition, e-mails, and advancement opportunities. The influence of recognition indicated its importance among the participants. For example, Participant 17 stated,

> I would say it's periodical. I'm not always looking for the pat on the back, but when you get rewarded, or just having someone give you a good comment or a good review about the work you've been doing, it's pretty gratifying.

It was also noted that recognition could be internally driven. Participant 4 replied, "I really feel like I am more of a servant, and that is what I feed off: making sure my guys are okay." Participant 5 stated, "I do like money, but that is not what incentivizes me. It's being successful in my own right. I like to accomplish something. It's what motivates me."

Eight participants agreed that verbal recognition was the most likely source of recognition. Participant 16 stated, "My general manager is on the floor. He's active. He's talking to people. I feel that I am recognized." Participant 12 mentioned, "I am recognized at least on a monthly basis in our shop and on conference calls and through our upper management." Out of the six participants who stated that they were not recognized, half stated they didn't mind not being recognized and they have to be self-motivated. Participant 8 stated,

> Sometimes, I have to be self-motivated because the company, itself, does not motivate their employees. That's something I try to bring across to them, and we've lost a lot of employees because of that, including myself. Sometimes it's disappointing because the employers are not motivated. I love my job and that's why I self-motivate myself.

The consensus was that recognition is beneficial, but not necessary. When leaders do not provide recognition, the participants acknowledged they would look for sources within themselves without too much concern about not being recognized. They appreciated recognition from any outlet.

3. Welcome High Level of Responsibility

The participants believed that they had a high level of responsibility. Eighteen out 20 participants thought they either had a high degree of responsibility or were overwhelmed with their current level of responsibilities. Participant 6 stated,

> I feel that I have a pretty high level of responsibility; a lot of it is a self-assigned responsibility as well that I just take on because I know I can figure things out. I think for my age I have a pretty high level of responsibility. I don't think I expected to be in this

position at this age when I was in college or anything like that, so I think I have a good level, but a lot of it like I said is self-assigned, like I take responsibility for things that maybe aren't technically in my realm, but I can assist with them, and I can provide that, so I do.

Participant 12 responded,

In my opinion on my level of responsibility is I love being part of the management crew. I love working with the team, directing the team. Felt like I have a good skill for it. I feel like I'm good with working under pressure. It is just like if you want something done right, you got to do it yourself.

Participated 11 asserted,

I've always been given a great deal of responsibility because I try to take on so much. I don't like to just sit by and not do anything, so I've always been handed off quite a bit of work, and I really enjoy having it.

As seen above, participants noted that they had a significant amount of responsibility. However, several individuals noted they took additional responsibilities on themselves because they felt they were the most capable of accomplishing the task correctly. The most frequent response was the responsibility was necessary and welcomed; however, there were times when the participants noted they took on too much. For example, Participant 5 mentioned,

My responsibility was way larger than my actual role entailed. I actually learned a lot from that. I was eager to take on that much stuff and probably would have responsibility, and it's been better to limit myself on how much I'm taking on. Suddenly now I've got too much responsibility, and it became hard to delegate out. My responsibility was gigantic; it was big.

The participants acknowledged that responsibility was a positive factor, even when responsibly was more than they could handle.

4. Lack of Future Growth Impacts Motivation

Questions 7 and 9 were influential in understanding the participants' status regarding advancement opportunities, as well as understanding if there were possibilities for further growth. Sixteen of 20 participants responded that they had opportunities for advancement since they were hired. Some participants had tremendous growth within their organization. For example, participant 6 stated, "So I have worked there for 6 years now and this is the fifth position I have held." Participate 12 stated, "I have already moved up three positions in the past 2 and a half years." Participant 5 mentioned, "The position I came into, I was three notches below where I ended up when I left."

The participants indicated concern about future opportunities for advancement. Ninety percent of the participants indicated that the possibility for further growth affects motivation either positively or negatively. As mentioned previously, most had already received advancement opportunities; however, participants reported that some of them felt that they had reached their ceiling for advancing within the organization. Forty-five percent of the participants indicated that the lack of advancement opportunities had affected their motivation negatively. Participant 18 stated,

> Well I've noticed recently I think it lowered my motivation because I know I'm already at the top level, and there's nowhere else to go from here. I'm one of those people that like to work hard to get to the top.

Participant 6 responded,

> We were actually just acquired by another company about the same size, just more of a merger, but they acquired us. And now with

their structure, they have less levels than we do so it's kind of on their side. They have a two-level gap missing compared to my company, so I don't see there is any way to go, and I'm not going to be an owner.

Participant 8 asserted, "I've actually looked into swapping careers or working for another company. I haven't gotten to that point yet. I've been there 13 years, so I'm afraid of losing seniority."

The possibility for further growth affected motivation in a positive way. A few of the participants expressed excitement for growth. Participant 11 stated,

They are always wanting us to learn more, to keep changing our methods, to be more outside the box to bring in new business. So there's always new positions for loan officers and for higher management.

Participant 9 mentioned,

The ability for growth, I could potentially get more territories underneath. I could possibly be in charge of more territories in my region and that is my goal for next year.

Some participants expressed the possibility for further growth with possible exceptions, meaning they are either not looking to grow with the current organization, they may be seeking to leave to another organization, or they may stay for a few more years.

5. Disconnect in Generational Gap

All 20 participants noted there is a disconnect within the generation gap between the millennial generation and the other the generations, including a disconnect between younger millennials and older millennials. First, I am going to illustrate the concern for the gap between millennials and other generations.

Participant 7 posited,

I hear a lot about discussions generally the lack of motivation maybe among millennials. Actually, the conversations yesterday discussing the fact that sometimes some of the younger employees don't necessarily want to put in the same amount of work it takes to get to a certain level, meaning they kind of walk into the role, expecting a promotion or expecting instant gratification without having to put in the work to build their reputation and move up in the organization.

Participant 4 asserted,

I noticed that millennials don't like to plan ahead, so it's hard to see how you can motivate other millennials. I think they just think they're all about themselves and my generation is very selfish and very entitled.

Participant 16 mentioned,

I feel that I'm not a millennial. I'm not a typical millennial. I definitely have worked really hard to get where I'm at. But, I have had people work under me that the code word would be entitled.

Participant 6 stated,

I actually read books on how to manage millennials, even know I am a millennial, so I actually feel that I identify more as the generation before me somehow which is kind of weird. It seems my boss was born 1980 or 1981, so he barely made the millennial cut too. I actually have a hard time managing them and feel that people outside of the millennial generation can actually relate to me just fine or better. I feel like it is odd because I'm 5 years into the millennial generation.

Participant 19 posited,

It's funny because I was a coach previously in college. Those girls were really close to my generation. I think as far as now as the millennials are coming up, I think a lot of it is an entitlement. A lot of them think they're entitled. It's going to be harder and harder I think to actually manage and supervise this millennial group of people coming up, because of the sense of entitlement. I feel like I'm a different generation of millennials.

The participants indicated there seems to be a disconnect between the millennial generation. According to the participants, there was a unanimous feeling of disconnection between other generations and the millennials. Participant 10 stated,

I don't think they quite understand our generation and they think that the same motivating factors that contributed to their success are the same factors that motivate us. It's actually quite different now.

Participant 19 mentioned,

I think that they think we are a bit lazier than their own generation. The biggest difference is the way we use technology in the workplace versus the way they come up in the workplace. Participant 4 stated, "I'm not really sure if they know what motivates us other than thinking that greed or profit."

Participant 2 asserted,

Baby boomers, they are more resistant to change, and I think it's based on the era in which they grew up. Participant 17 responded, "They're kind of still stuck in their times. A lot of them don't want to conform to using email, but there are some that definitely try to get the grasp of it." Participant 13 mentioned,

Some of the generations think we're inherently lazy or don't like the approach we take to things. I feel they are set in their ways. Participant 20 responded, "I think that with the millennial generation, it's more about praise and being positive and giving feedback real time. Whereas with other generation, it was just solely a business model."

The consensus from the participants was not only the fact that there was a disconnect from other generations when compared to the millennial generation, but the disconnect was also concerning between younger and older millennials.

6. The Aspect of Work is Important

Millennials had a positive outlook on work and received high remarks for work in general. Ninety percent of the participants viewed work in a positive light and responded with their opinions about the importance of. Participant 9 stated, "As far as my job, I love it. I love helping clean the environment and helping other people; also being able to give back and helping people that work underneath me to reach their goals." Participant 19 responded, "I think it's just part of life's natural path is working. You go to work to go home and provide for the things that you want in life." Participant 11 stated,

I really enjoy working, and I like to try to just do the best job that I can. I think it's really important, even if it's a job you don't really like doing very well, that you give it your all. Participant 15 responded, I think that work is the oxygen of success. you cannot achieve success without work. I think it's critical and there's no way around it, period. The participants noted in a show of emotion that work was important to them and they connected work to being a positive part of life.

7. Importance of Achievement

All 20 participants provided an in-depth dialogue of their achievements. The accomplishments range from achieving personal goals, including advancement opportunities, exceeding company standards, helping clients, and giving back to the community. Forty percent of the participants achieved self-actualization, while others emphasized sales, marketing, customer service, and community involvement as being an essential part of achievement. Participant 6 stated,

I have changed and shaped our corporate culture as I have traveled through multiple departments. I help shaped the company culture. Participant 7 responded, "I hold the record for sales in the company. I have implemented all kind of processes that have improved, increased revenue and improved customer interaction."

According to Participant 17,

I've sealed some pretty good deals, like at least $10,000 projects, and those are key relationships that you like to establish for years to come. Participant 15 responded, "I am a business leader in the industry, in the community, so a lot of my accomplishments have ranged from helping people with their business goals."

Each participant was asked to identify adjectives to describe themselves as a millennial leader. Approximately 35% of the adjectives provided by the participants focused on moving forward and progressing with goals. The words included driven, focused, ambitious, hard-working, determined, competitive, go-getter, and goal-oriented. Close to 25% of participants mentioned the ability to have personal values that matter in their achievement, including understanding, honest, compassionate, friendly, a communicator, loyal, and a listener.

Participant 1 stated,

I would say aggressive career wise. You could probably say that ambitious is a little different. I would like to think of it as aggressive as I'm going to go get the job that I want rather than wait for the job to come to me.

Participant 18 noted,

Being a leader, I like to help people reach their goals be it large or small, means them exceeding in the company that they work for or whether it is more of a personal goal for them. I like to get everyone to succeed in what they do. Unfortunately, not one of us likes to fire people but sometimes it is a better use of their time in another space.

Participant 2 replied,

> I consider myself to be a go-getter. I like to set the pace; I am not a follower. I move it. In that respect, you try to go outside of the box and to put myself in a situation where I would be taking more of a leadership role and enhancing and enforcing that work with me or my subordinates.

Participant 14 mentioned,

> The first thing that comes to mind is to lead by example. I'm not an authoritarian, and I think that's pretty common among my generation. It's no more a lead decree. It's much more of a collaborative, "let me take you under my wing," "let me take you on as a mentor," "let me see what you think." It's not so authoritarian, like I was saying. That is the biggest thing with me. I like to lead people.

The seven themes demonstrated the core commonalities shared by the participants and the ways they viewed the traits that were important to them as millennial leaders. The data accumulated from the themes helped provide a comprehensive framework to answer the research questions. The results of the research questions indicated the participants answered honestly, and I analyzed the data in an attempt to ensure credibility and trustworthiness.

While developing the seven important themes that help understand retain and motivate millennial leadership, the participants also help determine answers to the following important research questions about the perception from millennial leadership on how they are managed by organizations

Research Question 1:

What are Generation Y leaders' lived experiences and

reactions when the leaders of service organizations try to motivate the teams to which they belong in the southwestern United States? The participants categorized millennials leading other millennials as different because the feedback demonstrated that a variation exists between millennials born earlier and millennials born later in the generation time frame. Participant 4 mentioned, "I noticed that millennials don't like to plan ahead, so it is hard to see how you can motivate other millennials."

Other reactions from the participants included the responses for being ambitious and focused on their careers, along with being empathetic. The participants understood that other generations such as baby boomers are not technically savvy in many ways. Participant 19 posited,

The biggest difference is the way we use technology in the workplace versus the way they come up in the workplace, especially for people who've been working at my job for years. Participant 16 responded, "I know I've had to help my older generational managers understand where the millennials are coming from."

The participants were quick to note their personal accomplishments, along with what they had achieved together with their teams. The teams included members of other generation in many cases. The millennials understood that they were aggressive in their careers, but they wanted help progress change and aid others. Participant 9 mentioned,

I personally like to see change I can make in the world, whether it be with one person or on a larger scale helping a child how to swim, helping a person advance in their career. I like to see the change and be the change. Participant 18 responded, "I like to be able to know how to motivate people and get them going, and what they're doing."

Millennials also recognized the importance of having fun, developing friendships, and being part of a community to focus on the processes and duties of the job. Participant 6 stated,

> I do recognize the concerns of millennials and I get it because I like it as well, focusing on activities or forming a community in the workplace as opposed to just being the boss. It's your job; you get a paycheck that should be sufficient. I guess that would be a fun atmosphere or whatever I guess you want to call it.

Participant 5 replied,

> I'm not an authoritarian, and I think that's common among my generation. It's no more a lead decree. It's much more of a collaborative, "let me take you under my wing," "let me take you on as a mentor," "let me show you how to do this," and "let me get your input," "let me see what you think." It's not so authoritarian, like I was saying. That is the biggest thing with me. I like to lead by example.

Participant 9 asserted,

> Being a leader, I like to help people reach their goals, be it large or small means them exceeding in the company that they work for, either with me or whether it is more of a personal goal for them. I like to get everyone succeeding in what they do.

Millennials also noted having to prove themselves as hard-working individuals because of the negative traits displayed by others who act lazy and entitled. The participants described the negative connotations referenced regarding millennials. Participant 12 mentioned,

> As a millennial leader, I feel that I'm trying to obviously prove something to myself as well as to others. Especially outside of the millennials because to an extent I feel like we have a rep or others feels like we were given a lot I should say. I feel like I have to always prove to every generation.

Research Question 2:

What factors are causing Generation Y leaders to leave service organizations? Responses indicated that three elements were apparent in leaving their current service organization that included compensation, Lack of growth, and Work-life balance. A good compensation package seemed to be a prerequisite for feeling adequately paid within their job. Lack of growth opportunities appeared to accompany leaving an organization. Finally, the lack of work and life balance was a cause for thinking about leaving an organization.

Over one third of the participants (35%) acknowledged that they did not feel fairly compensated. A few of the participants thought their age was a contributing factor for having a lower wage than their counterparts had. For example, Participant 8 stated, "The only turnaround there is I also know what others get paid. Like I said, sometimes it's unfair. I think it's due to my age and my gender [female]." Participant 10 stated, "I think my age contributes a lot to why I'm making what I make. All my 'equal counterparts' make at least 25% to 30% more than I do."

Almost 45% of the participants who did not feel satisfied with their compensation were looking to leave their current position. Participant 19 stated,

> It affects me a lot because I want to move up to that point where I feel like, the work I'm doing, I'm being financially compensated for. At this point, when we're not being compensated the way we are, I sign up for overtime or I pick up extra shifts to make sure I'm getting to the financial point that I need to be at.

The opportunity for growth was a significant concern among the participants, as 45% believed they had reached the high point at their current job or they perceived there were no opportunities and would likely leave their companies sooner rather than later. Twenty-five percent of participants perceived there was no further opportunity for growth, and 35% of the participants perceived there were growth opportunities with exceptions. For example, Participant 18 stated, "I'm already at the top level, and there is nowhere else to go from there. I'm one of those people that like to work hard and get to the top." Participant 6 stated,

> So, I was kind of sticking around, waiting for that opportunity. I don't know. I am going to be stuck now and you know I don't have any big jobs to look forward to, so that is something I am looking at and considering.

The lack of opportunities for growth including those participants that articulated that 45% believed that this impacted their motivation negatively, while an additional 15% of participants had mixed emotions and were not sure of the impact, but were concern there could be negative impact.

> The ability to manage a work and life balance was a concern. Thirty percent of the participants indicated that they had too much to do and were unable to have that balance or they had yet to find out how to manage. Participant 19 stated,

> I fairly struggle with that one a little bit. I probably work a lot more than I should. Where I am in my life right now, my husband and I both work so many hours. It's just crazy that we don't spend enough time together outside the work. We're still young.

Participant 16 replied,

> It's actually a conversation I planned on having with my boss, because I literally talked to my boyfriend yesterday, I said, "Whatever it was that happened last week, nothing specifically that triggered it, it just made me think. Okay, in the next 2 to 3 years, if we plan on getting married, it will happen around then. Another year from then or so, I have a kid. Can I still be working these hours? And do what I do?" Participant 8 mentioned, "It's difficult

sometimes because they also interfere with your personal life. After 13 years of serving them, in those 13 years, I have not gone on vacation and not taken my laptop with me. I leave on vacation and I take my laptop from wherever I'm at."

Research Question 3:

What role does employer motivation play in the retention of Generation Y leaders in the service industry? The role of employer motivation included a positive or negative outcome in several areas according to the participants. Participants noted in the interviews that they were recognized in a variety of ways that included their boss verbally communicating or communicating via e-mail or by providing monetary compensation. Participant 12 stated, "I am actually, yes. I am recognized a least on a monthly basis in our shop and on conference calls and through our upper management." Participant 5 responded, "I would say, number one, people will tell me that, 'Hey you're really great at this,' 'Hey you're real great at that.' 'We're glad to have you on because since you have come on, we did this and that.'"

However, employers who do not recognize their employees can act as de-motivators according to participants or they have used their inner motivation to fill the void. Participant 7 posited,

> I would like to add people don't recognize how far acknowledgment goes, even more than compensation. I think that just knowing that you're a valued employee, knowing that what you're doing is noticed by your peers and by your manager is really important. I hear time and again from my employees and I know I feel that way myself, so that is one thing I would like to add.

Participant 3 replied,

> It does somewhat impact my motivation when I'm not recognized as you expect that to be sort of the, not to say the main focus, but

one of the focuses of my employers to actually acknowledge the work that I have put into my job. In the same time, I would expect my employer to let me know when I'm not fulfilling my obligations, as they certainly do that. So, clearly I would expect them to acknowledge me when I am fulfilling my obligations or exceeding them.

Participant 7 responded,

It can be frustrating sometimes and there are days that I could really use that. But what I have found is that I need to find motivation in myself rather than trying to find external validation. That is how I deal with it.

Participant 8 stated,

Sometimes I have to be self-motivated because the company, itself, does not motivate their employees. That's something that I try to bring across to them and we've lost a lot of employees because of that. Including myself, sometimes it's disappointing because the employers are not motivated. I love my job and that's why I self-motivate myself, but coming from the employer, it doesn't come quite often.

In addition to acknowledgment being an important factor that millennial leaders identified, they also mentioned the generation gap because the same motivation factors that contributed to others' success in previous generations are not the same factors for the millennial generation. Participant 10 stated,

No. I don't they quite understand our generation and they think that the same motivating factors that contributed to their success are the same factors that motivate us. It's actually quite different now.

Participant 5 replied,

No. Yes. This is kind of an interesting topic. My uncle actually runs the consulting firm focusing on generational gaps on what motivates each generation, what each generation likes, and I think that is not only towards my generation but towards every generation. They believe they think they know what motivates the generation, and they kind of believe in it that way. Number one, it's hard to really, it's a stigma for the people. Number two, it's often wrong, even where there is a good generalization that could be accurately placed. It's often wrong. So yes.

When the participants stated that there was a belief that members of other generations understood what factors motivated millennial leaders, it was more that they were making an effort more than acknowledging outright. For example, Participant 12 stated,

> I guess yes to an extent. I feel like any other generation other than mine, other than the millennial generation that I work with, understand, at least me personally, where I'm coming from and what I'm trying to achieve, but I don't think that they really know to its fullest extent because of their generation. It's obviously completely different in what they have grown from than we have in my generation.

This section included a detailed analysis of the lived experiences of 20 millennial leaders who oversee subordinates in the service industry. The participants provided in-depth answers that contained their rich experiences. The participants provided insight into how others view millennials, along with how they view their career progression and their experiences as millennial leaders. The specific experiences of the participants and their perceptions emerged via the transcripts and provided an innovative perspective about the lived experiences of the 20 millennial leaders. The following themes emerged from the transcribed data and related to the research questions: work and life balance are important, recognition of work can be helpful, welcome high level of responsibility, lack of future growth impacts motivation, disconnect in generational gap, the aspect of work is important, and importance of achievement. In summary, the millennial leaders were eager to share their experiences about their journey in their career progression.

11 FINAL DETERMINATION

The discussions earlier in this book pointed to millennials taking more chances to leave their current employment for new job opportunities, and my research confirmed that millennials leaders are looking for advancement opportunities. If the possibilities for advancement are not available in their present organization, then the millennial leaders would look elsewhere. My research indicated that millennial leaders focus on and feel driven to achieve personal goals. If the goals of a company do not align with the goals of millennial leaders, then the millennial leaders will pursue other ways to achieve their goals. Employee turnover is a significant concern for millennial leaders. Some of the findings from the interview illuminated the concerns that millennials leaders have and why they would decide to leave their current organization.

The information provided encompassed key points, including that millennials desire to receive recognition as partners rather than in the top-down hierarchy of management. The findings confirmed this, as millennial leaders desired to have good relationships with their bosses and expected to be treated as an equal when they achieved at a high level within the organization. The findings also indicated that the majority of the participants appreciated having more responsibilities, which is synonymous with the desire to advance via promotions.

The results confirmed the importance of job satisfaction for millennial leaders in their current position. A critical area of concern to millennial leaders was work and life balance. Seventy percent of the participants acknowledged they had a good work and life balance, and 10% of the participants admitted part of the problem was they attempted to take on too much responsibility because they believed they were capable.

The research indicated that work imbalance could cause dissatisfaction among millennial leaders due to intense working conditions. However, millennial leaders seemed to feel more satisfied when they had increased responsibilities. The general response was the extra responsibilities encompassed job fulfillment through the idea that increased responsibility meant they felt accomplished in their occupational role. Ninety percent of the participants indicated they felt satisfied with the work they did.

The information reflected the concern that millennials were difficult to retain in the workforce. The problem demonstrated was that millennials had received the label of job hoppers, especially if they were not gaining the skills needed to increase their growth opportunities in their career. The study findings included the same responses about the need to advance and learn new skills. The majority of the participants had at least experienced one promotion at their current job. Even though the participants had received advancement opportunities, 50% of the participants acknowledged they still had potential for further advancement. The information in the research indicated that 90% of participants agreed that the possibility for further growth is a concern, and 50% of those participants stated the lack of future growth opportunities affects them negatively. The findings confirmed that millennial leaders, like millennials in general, need the chance to grow in their skills or at their current place of employment. It will be difficult to retain millennial leaders if they do not feel that their organization considers their best interests with regard to career advancements. The consensus of the study was the participants felt driven to succeed and were go-getters who would find what they were looking forward if the company leaders were unwilling to offer it.

Several participants mentioned the words entitled and entitlement during the interviews as either a misconception by other generations or a concern for millennials. Generations outside of millennials have labeled members of the millennial generation as entitled. However, the findings from the study indicated that some millennial leaders agreed that entitlement is a concern. Participant 4 mentioned, "I think they're all about themselves and my generation is very selfish and very entitled." Participate 15 posited,

> I think when it comes to seeing the differences between generations and getting those experiences, such as the changes in social media, the changes in trends about what millennials are really motivated to do. I guess kind of understanding what people refer to as a sense of entitlement.

Participant 1 replied,

> They just want to jump to that promotion and they think that they just do a little bit more than what was required by their job and therefore they are now entitled to another promotion.

The factors that motivated millennial leaders seemed to align with Maslow's hierarchy of needs, Herzberg's two-factor theory, Vroom's expectancy theory, and Adams's equity theory. I will highlight comparisons to the findings from the participants' responses. There were only a few differences regarding the conceptual framework outlined in Chapter 3.

Concerning Maslow's hierarchy of needs, 40% of the participants responded that their work had encompassed self-actualization because they felt personal satisfaction. To reach the status of self-actualization, participants would have felt they had achieved success, which means self-actualization is a benefit to society because it leads to more solidarity, care, problem solving, altruism, and compassion (Gurin & D'Souza, 2016). Most of the participants indicated that if they had more responsibility, they could do more. Self-actualization for the participants did not seem to resonate with having a large salary, bigger or better offices, or more job security. For example, all participants indicated their working conditions were either fair or good or they were not concerned. Few participants indicated they had concerns about Maslow's lower level needs; they believed they had accomplished significant goals or were going to do so soon. Many of the participants also asserted that they do want to do more or want more in their current employment positions.

Herzberg's two-factory theory encompassed the hygiene or dissatisfaction of employees or the motivation that included the satisfaction of the employee. The elements of dissatisfaction, according to Herzberg (1974), include job security, procedures, salary, and working conditions. None of the participants indicated that job security was a concern. There were some concerns regarding the administration of policies, but nothing indicated dissatisfaction by the participants. Salary was not a significant concern to the millennial leaders. Thirty-five percent of the participants indicated that they did not receive fair pay, while 25% stated pay affects their motivation. Participant 10 reported, "There are times when I feel like it's not worth staying but, but I have a really good relationship with the president." Only one participant reported leaving an employer due to compensation: "For me, I'm headed towards better money. That is another reason I'm leaving the company and going back to the financial industry where I feel like my work will be compensated a lot better than my current position." (Participant 12).

The participant's answers throughout were more indicative of the motivation part of Herzberg's two-factor theory. The factors that were of concern to the participants were achievement, advancement, responsibility, and growth opportunities. These predominant factors influenced whether they would stay with their current organization or look for new employment. Ninety percent of the participants indicated that future growth affected their motivation in either a positive or a negative direction. Growing with the organization influenced participants' motivation in a positive way. However, if the participant either was not progressing or had reached a progression plateau, the effect was negative. Participant 11 stated,

> They are always wanting us to learn more, to keep changing our methods, to be more think outside the box to bring in new business, so there are new positions. So there are other advancements I can do in my field currently.

Herzberg's motivation aspects of the two-factor theory compared to Maslow's hierarchy of needs, specifically in accordance to a level of high achievement. The ability to achieve and accomplish is an important part of self-recognizing. Participants asserted they had achieved many goals and believed they were an important asset to the organization because of what they had accomplished. The accomplishments included self-satisfaction for helping others, increasing profitability, transforming the company's culture, and identifying different improvement programs for their organization. Herzberg noted the importance of responsibility as an important aspect of motivation. Ninety percent of the participants believed they had a high level of responsibility that was within their capabilities, while 17% of that same group asserted their responsibility level was overwhelming.

Advancement opportunities were a significant part of the participants' motivation to stay with their organization, along with being a large part of their job satisfaction. Eighty percent of the participants stated that they had received at least one advancement at their current organization. However, even though they had received a promotion, participants indicated concern that if they did not continue to receive additional advancement opportunities, they might pursue other options. Participant 20 stated,

> I am always wanting to do more, learn more, be better and continue to grow and exceed my own goals and expectations. There is nowhere for me to continue to go. I get stuck and I feel like I need to look for something else.

The perception of the interviews as part of Herzberg's two-factor theory was significant concerning the satisfaction displayed by participants for achievement, advancement, responsibility, and growth opportunities, which demonstrated the essential traits that resonated with their response. The hygiene factor or sense of dissatisfaction if the participants were lacking was not a concern. According to Herzberg's theory, the participants did not show concern because they did not have a sense of dissatisfaction. The factors that motivated millennial leaders aligned with Herzberg's two-factor theory.

Millennial leaders, as well as other aspiring individuals, want to see their efforts rewarded, as demonstrated by the outliers of Vroom's expectancy theory. The basis of the expectancy theory is the groundwork that a person believes the perceived probability of exerting a given amount of effort will lead to achieving high performance. Thus, the participants expected to receive a reward when they met their goals. The findings of the research were consistent with the expectancy theory in many ways, although a few participants mentioned that they do not always receive recognition, but intrinsic motivation or recognition beyond their immediate supervisor was important for overcoming any lack of appreciation.

Adams's equity theory had many of the same characteristics as Herzberg's two-factory theory and Vroom's expectancy theory. Adams's equity theory acknowledges many of the same factors that affect the working relationship between employers and employees. When people receive fair treatment, they are likely to feel more motivated. The premise of the equity theory is to maintain a balance between the inputs within a job and the outputs received. The concern is an employee can feel de-motivated if the inputs outweigh the outputs. The equity theory was consistent with the participants' acknowledgment of their efforts, advancement opportunities, and growth within the organization.

Millennial leaders' descriptions through identifiers revolved around adjectives that described themselves through relative input terms like honest, hardworking, loyal, effort, adaptability. The same descriptive adjectives resonated with the inputs characterized by the terms of Adams's equity theory. The participants described the outputs achieved due to the inputs asserted, which included recognition and praise, increased responsibility, and advancement and growth opportunities, along with virtually no concern for job security.

The results demonstrated a disconnect between millennial leaders and other generations. All the participants asserted that there was a disconnect between millennials and other generations. Many of the concerns about what other generation cohorts thought about the millennials were consistent with information presented in earlier chapters. The research findings indicated that many millennials believe a generation difference exists between younger and older millennials.

Besides the generation gap between other generation cohorts, the research findings indicated that 25% of the participants posited that there were also differences between millennials born closer to 2000 compared to those born in the early 1980s. Participant 6 stated,

> Even know I am a millennial, I feel that I identify more like the generation before me somehow, which is kind of weird. It seems my boss was born in 1980 or 1981, so he barely made the millennial cut too. I actually have a hard time managing them and feel that people outside of the millennial generation can relate to me just fine or better. I feel it is odd because I'm 5 years into the millennial's generation.

Participant 16 responded,

> I feel the older generation of millennials are a different breed than some of the new younger ones. Perfect example: My boss hired this one guy that was 23-ish. He got his first paycheck and legitimately cried as to how much taxes were taken out and turned to my boss, as I sit right next to him, "Can you create a position like hers and pay me the same?" I wanted to punch him in the face.

Participant 20 mentioned,

> I feel the term millennial is a little too widespread. I was born in 1981 and I feel like that cutoff may be 1980, 1981; 1982 is really pushing it. I feel like there's people that were born a little bit after me that I really look at them and say, "I really hate to hire these people." They are millennials, and I have to tell them, "Thank you for coming to work," because it's their job. I think maybe the range that has been set there for the millennials is maybe not accurate.

Participant 10 asserted,

> It's a stereotype of millennial children. I think kids and teens born at the end of the 90s, early 2000, with the sudden and boom of the wave of technology. I think that would fit more in that generalization than those born early 1980s, or even up to 1995.

There seemed to be a firm belief by those millennial leaders not directed by a specific questioning that there were differences between millennials born in the early 1980s and millennials born in the late 1990s. At least 25% of the participants did not necessarily agree with the specific year guidelines in accordance with the generation theory, as noted in the answers to the interview questions. More participants may have agreed there was a difference if the interview included specific questions about the possible generational differences of older versus younger millennials.

The data acquired from the millennial leaders may improve the ability to understand and improve the experiences of millennial leaders in the service area. The significance and the results of the research contribute to the knowledge base about millennial leaders and their motivation factors. The study may be significant to large and small business employers, managers, and millennial leaders with regard to satisfaction, motivation, and retention. The participants in this study described what was important to them, how they can feel satisfied and retained in the workforce, and how employers can help them meet their goals and ambitions.

With millennial leaders becoming the dominant generation that will likely lead the majority of corporations in the near future as CEO's, President of divisions, etc., it is important to understand these leaders. It will be important to all business owners to find out what satisfies and motivates millennial leadership. The research findings in my research study were a clear indication of what is necessary to retain top millennial talent. An improved understanding from employers and corporations that employ millennial leaders, along with those who interact with millennial leaders will benefit by understanding what is important to millennial leaders via this study. The results of the study indicated there was a disconnect with other generations, as well as within the millennial generation, so it is important that members of the different generations have the ability to understand what makes the millennial generation feel satisfied and what defines success.

Participants statements on how they view being a millennial in the workforce where original perceptions are likely different than expected. It is crucial to understand what is important to the millennial leader and how they value work and their surrounding area. The millennial generation is a generation that has different needs and an intrinsic drive to succeed. Millennial leaders, to some degree, are an extension of the millennials as a whole. However, there were notable differences in the answers provided by the participants and in the information presented in the literature about the millennial generation.

The focus of the research was to explore the effect of motivation on employee retention for Generation Y cohort leaders in the service industry in the southwestern United States. The participants provided valuable information that helped identify what they valued within their career progression and the organization they were employed with while proving information on what is important to millennial leaders. The information provided has armed organizations with the tools to improve organizational development with a thorough understanding to what the values of Generation Y leaders are. We now know what the keys are to satisfying and retaining millennial leaders.

The results indicated that millennials valued advancement and further growth, as well as feeling satisfied with their work. The meaning of their work is important because it allows Millennial leaders to connect with their work and their causes that stem from work in many cases. This is different compared to the baby boom generation, in that they would rather work for one employer and experience a sense of job fulfillment and stability versus risking job stability. However, millennials are willing to make decisions that will enhance their advancement and growth opportunities while risking job stability.

Job stability is not the issue since Gen Y leaders are still advancing their careers and finding meaning from their work. Other examples of finding meaning through work is when millennial leaders are recognized for a job well done. I know this is where all the participation trophy jokes occur. However, it was imperative in my discussions that millennials are not looking for rewards for work that is not finished or completed at a low level. The expectation is that they receive recognition when they provide a high level of work and it should receive the proper notoriety by their immediate supervisor. This should be standard protocol for strong team culture.

Millennial Leaders also noted the welcoming of high-level responsibility. This does not include dumping unmeaningful work on their lap because it is convenient and self-serving. Millennial leaders are expecting that their supervisors will have the emotional intelligence to provide a high level of responsibility to prepare them for potential promotions. Gen Y leaders believe that receiving these opportunities demonstrate value to the organization. Meaning, these opportunities provide increased internal motivation to continue with the organization when Gen Y needs are being met.

Another concerning area that the completed research determined included how lack of future growth impacts motivation. The lack of learning new skills or being an integral part of the team can be received by the millennial leader as kicking them out the door since they are not appreciated or the perception of not being appreciated. Promotion opportunities are a focal point for millennials leaders during their career journey and will not be compromised by any organization because they understand their skill level to compete at a high level with their peers.

The results included concern for how members of other generations do not understand the millennial generation. The finding also indicated that older millennials born in the early 1980s viewed younger millennials born in the mid-to-late 1990s as entitled and much different from themselves with respect to their working habits. At times, the participants acknowledged that the fact that members of other generations view them from a negative perspective causes them some concern. They hear many of the same stigmas that follow the generation, including being lazy, entitled, and selfish.

The importance of achievement was noted as being highly favorable during the study. Generation Y leaders desire to know that the work that they identified with was helping the greater cause. The meaning of the work was a validation of their achievement by understanding the overall importance. For example, your job is to produce 100 widgets per hour. This does not seem so important, but when you hear, your job is to produce 100 widgets an hour and you will save lives. Now, a millennial leader can derive the importance of achievement by the meaning of their work. Many of the participants also discussed openly the importance of achieving company goals, in returned they felt like they were a bigger part of the organization because of their contributions.

The millennial generation is likely the most unique and misunderstood group in the workforce. I highlighted important areas that illuminate opportunities to engage, motivate, and retain millennial leaders in the workplace by providing advancement opportunities, additional responsibilities, and a proper work–life balance while increasing growth and learning opportunism and recognizing their work. By understanding the generation gap and using key indicators from this research to improve retention, organization leaders can learn how to accommodate and mentor members of the millennial generation to decrease the attrition rate of millennial leaders.

Overall, the millennial leadership generation is a tenacious group that values opportunities, relationships, appreciation and the willingness to achieve at a high level. This was believed to be a misunderstood generation; however, once each participant derived their story and discussed the key points to why they make up this generation, they are not so much misunderstood as the general public is misguided because of their own generation. Each generation represents different values depending on parental guidance and technology. Generation Z is now in the workforce and this group is also very different than millennials and those generations that preceded them.

Moving forward, you should be better prepared to understand, motivate, and retain millennial leaders. The important elements of this book includes the seven priority themes for Generation Y. The book also provides a solid foundation about previous generations which included baby boomers and Generation X. It was also important to provide an extensive background on retention and motivation to comprehend the foundation of each that enabled capturing of the key elements for millennial leaders and what was important to them. Of course, the book also provides an in-depth focus about the foundation of millennials, so we can better understand their personal growth patterns that have transcended into leadership roles within our organizations. Together, let's win over the next generation of leaders!

REFERENCES

Acar, A. B. (2014). Do intrinsic and extrinsic motivation factors differ for Generation X and Generation Y? *International Journal of Business and Social Science, 5*(5), 12-20. Retrieved from http://ijbssnet.com

Achim, I. M., Dragolea, L., & Balan, G. (2013). The importance of employee motivation to increase organizational performance. *Annales Universitatis Apulensis: Series Oconomica, 15*, 685-691. Retrieved from http://www.oeconomica.uab.ro

Adams, J. S. (1965). Inequity in social exchange. In L. Berkowitz (Ed.), *Advances in experimental social psychology* (Vol. 2, pp. 267-299). New York, NY: Academic Press.

Adams, J. S., & Jacobsen, P. R. (1964). Effects of wage inequities on work quality. *Journal of Abnormal and Social Psychology, 69*, 19-25. doi:10.10.1037/h0040241

Akila, R. (2012). A study on employee retention among executives at BGR Energy Systems LTD, Chennai. *International Journal of Marketing, Financial Services & Management Research, 1*(9), 18-32. Retrieved from http://indianresearchjournals.com

Armache, J. (2012). Effect of compensation and other motivational techniques on organizational productivity. *Franklin Business & Law Journal, 1*, 88-96. Retrieved from https://www.franklinpublishing.net

Aruna, M., & Anitha, J. (2015). Employee retention enablers: Generation Y employees. *SCMS Journal of Indian Management 12*(3), 94. Retrieved from http://www.scms.edu.in/JIM/

Baker, S. E., & Edwards, R. (2012). How many qualitative interviews is enough? Retrieved from National Centre for Research Methods website: http://eprints.ncrm.ac.uk

Beekman, T. (2011). Fill in the generation gap. *Strategic Finance, 93*(3), 15-17. Retrieved from http://www.imanet.org

Berson, Y., Halevy, N., Shamir, B., & Erez, M. (2015). Leading from different psychological distances: A construal-level perspective on vision communication, goal setting, and follower motivation. *Leadership Quarterly, 26*, 143-155. doi:10.1016/j.leaqua.2014.07.011

Blotnicky, K. A., Mann, L. L., & Joy, P. R. (2015). An assessment of university students healthy eating behaviors with the expectancy theory. *ASBBS E-Journal, 11*, 31. Retrieved from http://asbbs.org

Brown, E. A., Thomas, N. J., & Bosselman, R. H. (2015). Are they leaving or staying: A qualitative analysis of turnover issues for Generation Y hospitality employees with a hospitality education. *International Journal of Hospitality Management, 46*, 130-137. doi:10.16/j.ijhm.2015.01.011

Brown, M. (2012). Responses to work intensification: Does generation matter? *International Journal of Human Resources Management, 23*, 3578-3595. doi:10.1080/09585192.21011.654348

Cahill, T. F., & Sedrak, M. (2012). Leading a multigenerational workforce: Strategies for attracting and retaining millennials. *Frontiers of Health Services Management, 29*, 3-15. Retrieved from https://ache.org/pubs/Frontiers/frontiers_index.cfm

Campione, W. A. (2014). The influence of supervisor race, gender, age, and cohort on millennials' job satisfaction. *Journal of Business Diversity,* *14,* 18-34. Retrieved from http://www.na-businesspress.com/jbdopen.html

Casad, S. (2012). Implications of job rotation literature for performance improvement practitioners. *Performance Improvement Quarterly, 25*(2), 27-41. doi:10.1002/peq.21118

Chand, M., & Tung, R. L. (2014). The aging of the world's population and its effects on global business. *Academy of Management Perspectives, 28,* 409-429. doi:10.5465/amp.2012.0070

Choi, Y. G., Kwon, J., & Kim, W. (2013). Effects of attitudes vs. experience of workplace fun on employee behaviors: Focused on Generation Y in the hospitality industry. *International Journal of Contemporary Hospitality Management, 25,* 410-427. doi:10.1108/09596111311311044

Chou, S. Y., & Pearson, J. (2012). Organizational citizenship behaviors in IT profession: An expectancy theory approach. *Management Research Review, 35,* 1170-1186. doi:10.1108/01409171211291282

Combes, J. (2013). Strategies for managing a generationally diverse workforce. *Hospitals & Health Networks, 87*(10), 46-56. Retrieved from http://www.hhnmag.com/

Costanza, D. P., Badger, J. M., Fraser, R. L., Severt, J. B., & Gade, P. A. (2012). Generational differences in work-related attitudes: A meta-analysis. *Journal of Business Psychology, 27,* 375-394. doi:10.1007/s10869-012-9259-4

Coulter, J. S., & Faulkner, D. C. (2014). The multigenerational workforce. *Professional Case Management, 19,* 46-51. doi:10.1097/ncm.0000000000000008

Damij, N., Levnajic, Z., Rejec, V. S., & Sukland, J. (2015). What motivates us for work. An intricate web of factors beyond money and prestige. *Plos ONE, 10*(7), 1-13. doi:10.137/journal.pone.0132641

Deepthi, U., & Baral, R. (2013). Understanding the role of generational differences in psychological contract fulfillment and its impact on employees' cognitive responses. *Review of HRM, 2*, 74-84. Retrieved from https://www.elsevier.com/journals/locate/hrmr

Dey, J. G., & Pierret, C. R. (2014, December). Independence for young millennials: Moving out and boomeranging back. *Monthly Labor Review*, 1-10. Retrieved from http://www.bls.gov/opub/mlr/2014/home.htm

Dimitriou, C. K., & Blum, S. C. (2015). An exploratory study of Greek millennials in the hotel industry: How do they compare to other generations. *International Journal of Global Business, 8*, 62-92. Retrieved from http://www.gsmi-ijgb.com

Duffy, R. D., Autin, K. L., & Bott, E. M. (2015). Work volition and job satisfaction: Examining the role of work meaning and person environment. *Career Development Quarterly, 63*, 126-140. doi:10.1002/cdq.12009

Dumitrescu, L., Cetina, I., & Pentescu, A. (2012). Employee feedback-condition for their retention and loyalty. *Romanian Journal of Marketing, 3*, 11-19. Retrieved from http://www.revistademarketing.ro/

Dwivedula, R., Bredillet, C., & Müller, R. (2015). Towards an understanding of work motivation in temporary organizations. *PM World Journal, 4*(9), 1-12. Retrieved from https://pmworldlibrary.net/

Dye, K., Mills, A. J., & Weatherbee, T. (2005). Maslow: Man interrupted: reading management theory in context. *Management Decision, 43*, 1375-1395. doi:10.1108/00251740510634921

Eastman, J. K., Lyer, R., Liao-Troth, S., Williams, D. F., & Griffin, M. (2014). The role of involvement on millennials' mobile technology behaviors: The moderating impact of status consumption, innovation, and opinion leadership. *Journal of Marketing Theory & Practice, 22*, 455-470. doi:10.2753/MTP1069-6679220407

Eberle, G. J. (1919). Labor turnover. *American Economic Review, 9*, 79. Retrieved from https://www.aeaweb.org/

Elias, S. M., Smith, W. L., & Barney, C. E. (2012). Age as a moderator of attitude towards technology in the workplace: Work motivation and overall job satisfaction. *Behaviour & Information Technology, 31*, 453-467. doi:10.1080/0144929x.2010.513419

Englander, M. (2012). The interview: Data collection in descriptive phenomenological human scientific research. *Journal of Phenomenological Psychology, 43*, 13-35. doi:10:1163/156916212X632943

Eversole, B. A., Venneberg, D. L., & Crowder, C. L. (2012). Creating a flexible organizational culture to attract and retain talented workers across generations. *Advances in Developing Human Resources, 14*, 607-625. doi:10.1177/1523422312455612

Farrell, L., & Hurt, A. C. (2014). Training the millennial generations: Implications for organizational climate. *Journal of Organizational Learning & Leadership, 12*, 47-60. Retrieved from http://www.leadingtoday.org/weleadinlearning/

Ferri-Reed, J. (2014a). Are millennial employees changing how managers manage? *Journal for Quality and Participation, 37*(2), 15-18, 35. Retrieved from http://asq.org

Ferri-Reed, J. (2014b). "Millennializing" the work environment. *Journal for Quality & Participation, 37*(4), 17-18. Retrieved from http://asq.org

Festing, M., & Schafer, L. (2014). Generational challenges to talent management: A framework for talent retention based on the psychological-contract perspective. *Journal of World Business, 49*, 262-

271. doi:10.1016/j.jwb.2013.11.010

Freeman, M. (2014). The hermeneutical aesthetics of thick description. *Qualitative Inquiry, 20*, 827-833. doi:10.177/1077800414530267

Friedell, K., Puskala, K., & Villa, N. (2011). *Hiring, promotion, and progress: Millennials' expectations in the workplace* (St. Olaf College Working Paper). Retrieved from http://www.kyrafriedell.com/wp-content/uploads/2014/02/SOAN-371-Final-Paper.pdf

Gentry, W. A., Griggs, T. L., Deal, J. J., Mondore, S. P., & Cox, B. D. (2011). A comparison of generational differences in endorsements of leadership practices with actual leadership skill level. *Consulting Psychology Journal: Practice and Research, 63*, 39-49. doi:10.1037/a0023015

Gibson, J. W., Greenwood, R. A., & Murphy, E. F., Jr. (2011). Generation difference in the workplace: Personal values, behaviors, and popular beliefs. *Journal of Diversity Management, 4*(3), 1-8. Retrieved from http://www.cluteinstitute.com/journals/journal-of-diversity-management-jdm/

Gilbert, J. (2011). The millennials: A new generation of employees, a new set of engagement policies. *Ivey Business Journal, 75*(5), 26-29. Retrieved from http://iveybusinessjournal.com

Goodman, E. (2015). Here comes the millennials: Are they ready to rent? *Journal of Property Management, 1*, 16-21. Retrieved from http://www.irem.org/jpm

Goudreau, J. (2013, January). Are millennials 'deluded narcissists'? *Forbes*, 1-3. Retrieved from https://www.forbes.com

Guess, H. S. (2014). Maslow's hierarchy of needs: The sixth level. *The Psychologist, 27*(12), 982-983. Retrieved from http://thepsychologist.bps.org.uk

Guetterman, T. C. (2015). Description of Sampling Practices Within Five

Approaches to Qualitative Research in Education and Health Sciences. *Qualitative Social Research, 16*(2), 1-3. Retrieved from http://www.qualitative-research.net/

Gupta, A., & Tayal, T. (2013). Impact of competing force of motivational factors on employees at workplace. *Information and Knowledge Management, 3*(5), 143-148. Retrieved from http://www.iiste.org

Gurin, M., & D'Souza, J. (2016). The universal significance of Maslow's concept of self-actualization. *The Humanistic Psychologist, 44*(2), 210-214. doi:10.1037/hum0000027

Hamori, M., Koyuncu, B., Cao, J., & Graf, T. (2015). What high-potential young managers want. *MIT Sloan Management Review, 57*, 61-68. Retrieved from http://www.sloanreview.mit.edu

Hansen, J.-I. C., & Leuty, M. E. (2012). Work values across generations. *Journal of Career Assessment, 20*, 34-52. doi:10.1177/1069072711417163

Hartman, L. J., & McCambridge, J. (2011). Optimizing millennials' communication styles. *Business and Professional Communication Quarterly, 4*, 22-44. doi:10.1111/1080569910395564

Hartmann, F. G., & Slapničar, S. (2012). Pay fairness and intrinsic motivation: The role of pay transparency. *International Journal of Human Resource Management, 23*, 4283-4300. doi:10.1080/09585192.2012.664962

Hartmann, N. N., & Rutherford, B. N. (2015). Psychological contract breach's antecedents and outcomes in salespeople: The roles of psychological climate, job attitudes, and turnover intention. *Industrial Marketing Management, 51*, 158-170. doi:10.1016/j.indmarman.2015.07.017

Hassard, J. S. (2012). Rethinking the Hawthorne studies: The Western Electric research in its social, political and historical context.

Human Relations, 65, 1431-1461. doi:10.1177?0018726712452168

Hauser, L. (2014). Work motivation in organizational behavior. *Economics, Management, and Financial Markets, 9*(4), 239-246. Retrieved from https://www.addletonacademicpublishers.com/89-economics-management-and-financial-markets

Hayyat, M. S. (2012). A study of relationship between leader behaviors and subordinate job expectancies: A path-goal approach. *Pakistan Journal of Commerce & Social Sciences, 6,* 357-371. Retrieved from http://pakacademicsearch.com

Helms, K. J. (2014, December 29). Millennials poised to become greatest entrepreneurial generation: Pay scout's global capabilities provide critical support and help manage risk. Retrieved from http://www.virtual-strategy.com

Hema Malini, P. H., & Washington, A. (2014). Employees' motivation and valued rewards as a key to effective QWL-from the perspective of expectancy theory. *TSM Business Review, 2*(2), 45. Retrieved from http://www.tsm.ac.in/LinkPageContent.aspx?Mid=68&PiD=0

Herzberg, F. (1974). The wise old Turk. *Harvard Business Review, 52*(5), 70-81. Retrieved from https://hbr.org

Hester, J. (2013). The high cost of employee turnover and how to avoid it. *Nonprofit World, 31,* 20-21. Retrieved from http://www.snpo.org/publications/ nonprofitworld.php

Hewlett, S. A., Sumberg, K., & Sherbin, L. (2009). How Gen Y & Boomers will reshape your agenda. *Harvard Business Review, 87*(7), 153. Retrieved from https://hbr.org

Hofmans, J., Gieter, S. D., & Pepermans, R. (2013). Individual differences in the relationship between satisfaction with job rewards and job satisfaction. *Journal of Vocational Behavior, 82,* 1-9. doi:10.1016/j.jvb.2012.06.007

Hokanson, C., Sosa-Fey, J., & Vinaja, R. (2011). Mitigating the loss of knowledge resulting from the attrition of younger generation employees. *International Journal of Business & Public Administration, 8,* 138-151. Retrieved from http://www.ijbssnet.com

Holm, T. T. (2012). Managing millennials: Coaching the next generation. *Forensic, 97*(2), 25-38. Retrieved from http://www.speechanddebate.org/pkd/

Holt, S., Marques, J., & Way, D. (2012). Bracing for the millennial workforce: Looking for ways to inspire Generation Y. *Journal of Leadership, Accountability & Ethics, 9*(6), 81-93. Retrieved from http://www.na-businesspress.com/jlaeopen.html

Hong, E. N. C., Hao, L. Z., Kumar, R., Ramendran, C., & Kadiresan, V. (2012). An effectiveness of human resource management practices on employee retention in institute of higher learning: A regression analysis. *CSC Journal, 3*(2), 60-79. Retrieved from http://theijmb.org

Howe, N., & Strauss, W. (1992, December). The new generation gap. *Atlantic,* 67+. Retrieved from http://www.atlanticmedia.com/

Irving, P. (2015). Self-empowerment in later life as a response to ageism. *Generations, 39,* 72-77. Retrieved from http://www.asaging.org

Islam, S. U., & Ali, N. (2013). Motivation-hygiene theory: Applicability on teachers. *Journal of Managerial Sciences, 7,* 87-104. Retrieved from http://www.qurtuba.edu

Ismail, M., & Lu, H. S. (2014). Cultural values and career goals of the millennial generation: An integrated conceptual framework. *Journal of International Management Studies, 9,* 38-49. Retrieved from http://www.jimsjournal.org

Ivtzan, I., Gardner, H. E., Bernard, I., Sekhon, M., & Hart, R. (2013). Wellbeing through Self-fulfilment: Examining developmental aspects of self-actualization. *Humanistic Psychologist, 41*, 119-132. doi:10.1080/08873267.2012.712076

Jerome, N. (2013). Application of the Maslow's hierarchy of need theory: Impacts and implications on organizational culture, human resource, and employee's performance. *International Journal of Business and Management Invention, 2*(3), 39-45. Retrieved from http://www.ijbmi.org

Johnson, J. M., & Ng, E. S. (2015, June). Money talks or millennials walk: The effect of compensation on nonprofit millennial workers' sector-switching intentions. *Review of Public Personnel Administration, 36*(3), 283-305. doi: 10.1177/0734371x15587980

Johnson, M. (2015). Stop talking about work/life balance! TEQ and the millennial generation. *Workforce Solutions Review, 6*(2), 4-7. Retrieved from http://ihrim.org

Kalman, F. (2012, March 20). How to 'millennialize' the office. Retrieved from http://www.talentmgt.com

Kapoor, C., & Solomon, N. (2011). Understanding and managing generational differences in the workforce. *Worldwide Hospitality and Tourism Themes, 3*, 308-318. doi:10.1108/17554211111162435

Kauri, V. (2013). The young and the restless. *Maclean's, 126*(45), 58-59. Retrieved from http://www.macleans.ca

Kellison, T. B., Yu Kyoum, K., & Magnusen, M. J. (2013). The work attitudes of millennials in collegiate recreational sports. *Journal of Park & Recreation Administration, 31*, 78-97. Retrieved from http://js.sagamorepub.com/

Kilber, J., Barclay, D., & Ohmer, D. (2014). Seven tips for managing Generation Y. *Journal of Management Policy & Practice, 15*(4), 80-91. Retrieved from http://www.jmppnet.com/

Kleiman, S. (2004). Phenomenology: To wonder and search for meanings.

Nurse Researcher, 11, 7-19. doi:10.7748/nr2004.07.11.4.7.c6211

Koltko-Rivera, M. E. (2006). Rediscovering the later version of Maslow's hierarchy of needs: Self-transcendence and opportunities for theory, research, and unification. Review of General Psychology, 10, 302-317. doi:10.1037/1089-2680.10.4.302

Korzynski, P. (2013). Employee motivation in new working environment. International Journal of Academic Research, 5(5), 184-188. doi:10.7813/2075-4124.2013/5-5/B.28

Kowske, B., Rasch, R., & Wiley, J. (2010). Millennials' (lack of) attitude problem: An empirical examination of generational effects on work attitudes. Journal of Business & Psychology, 25, 265-279. doi:10.1007/s10869-010-9171-8

Kraimer, M. L., Shaffer, M. A., Harrison, D. A., & Ren, H. (2012). No place like home? An identity strain perspective on repatriate turnover. Academy of Management Journal, 55, 399-420. doi:10.5465/amj-2009.0644

Kralj, A., Kandampully, J., & Sonet, D. (2012). Generation Y employees: An examination of work attitude differences. Journal of Applied Management and Entrepreneurship, 17(3), 36-54. Retrieved from http://www.whitneypress.com

Kuhl, J. S. (2014). Investing in millennials for the future of your organization. Leader to Leader, 71, 25-30. Retrieved from http://www.leadertoleaderjournal.com

Kulchmanov, A., & Kaliannan, M. (2014). Does money motivate employees? Empirical study of private and public financial sector in Kazakhstan. International Journal of Business and Management, 9(11), 214-223. Retrieved from http://www.theijbm.com

Kulik, C. T., Ryan, S., Harper, S., & George, G. (2014). Aging populations and management. Academy of Management Journal, 57, 929-935.

doi:10.5465/amj.2014.4004

Kultalahti, S., & Viitala, R. L. (2014). Sufficient challenges and a weekend ahead: Generation Y describing motivation at work. *Journal of Organizational Change Management, 27*, 569-582. doi:10.1108/JOCM-05-2014-0101

Lacey, M. Y., & Groves, K. (2014). Talent management collides with corporate social responsibility: Creation of inadvertent hypocrisy. *Journal of Management Development, 33*, 399-409. doi:10.118/JMD-06-2012-0073

Lacey, R., Kennett-Hensel, P., & Manolis, C. (2015). Is corporate social responsibility a motivator or hygiene factor. *Journal of the Academy of Marketing Science, 43*, 315-332. doi:10.1007/s11747-014-0390-09-9

Lai, S. L., Chang, J., & Hsu, L. Y. (2012). Does effect of workload on quality of work life vary with generations? *Asia Pacific Management Review, 17*, 437-451. doi:10.6126/APMR.2012.17.4.06

Laird, M., Harvey, P., & Lancaster, J. (2015). Accountability, entitlement, tenure, and satisfaction in Generation Y. *Journal of Managerial Psychology, 30*, 87-100. doi:10.1108/JMP-08-2014-0227

Lancaster, L. C., & Stillman, D. (2002). *When generations collide: Who they are, why they clash, how to solve the generation puzzle at home.* New York, NY: Harpers Collins.

Lazaroiu, G. (2015). Work motivation and organizational behavior. *Contemporary Readings in Law and Social Justice 7(2),* 66-75. Retrieved from http://heinonline.org

Levoy, B. (2014). The many benefits of job enrichment. *Podiatry Management, 33*(5), 77-78. Retrieved from http://www.podiatrym.com

Liu, D., Mitchell, T. R., Lee, T. W., Holtom, B. C., & Hinkin, T. R. (2012). When employees are out of step with coworkers: How job satisfaction trajectory and dispersion influence individual and unit voluntary turnover. *Academy of Management Journal, 55*, 1360-1380. doi:10.5465/amj.2010.0920

Liu, H., & Han, L. (2013). The beauty of transcending of the humanity: Research on Maslow's self-actualization theory. *International Conference on Advances in Social Science, Humanities, and Management, 13,* 229-233. doi:10.2991/asshm-13.2013.42

Lowe, D., Levitt, K. J., & Wilson, T. (2011). Solutions for retaining Generation Y employees in the workplace. *IEEE Engineering Management Review, 39*(2), 46-52. doi:10.1109/emr.2011.5876174

Luscombe, J., Lewis, J., & Biggs, H. C. (2013). Essential elements for recruitments and retention: Generation Y. *Education + Training, 55*(3) 272-290. doi:10.1108/00400911311309323

Malik, M. A. R., Butt, A. N., & Choi, J. N. (2015). Rewards and employee creative performance: Moderating effects of creative self-efficacy, reward importance, and locus of control. *Journal of Organizational Behavior, 36*, 59-74. doi:10.1002/job.1943

Mannheim, K. (1952). The sociological problem of generations. In P. Kecskemeti (Ed.), *Essays on the sociology of knowledge*, 276-322. London, England: Routledge. Retrieved from http://www.scirp.org/

Marston, C. (2007). *Motivating the" what's in it for me" workforce: Manage across the generational divide and increase profits.* Hoboken, NJ: J. John Wiley & Sons.

Maslow, A. H. (1943). A theory of human motivation. *Psychological Review, 50*, 370-396. Retrieved from http://www.apa.org/pubs/journals

Maslow, A. H. (1970). *Motivation and personality* (3rd ed.). New York, NY: Harper & Row.

McGinley, J., Weese, T., Thompson, J., & Leahy, K. (2011). Intelligence community assessment: Generational differences in workplace motivation. *American Intelligence Journal, 29*, 80-87. Retrieved from http://www.nmia.org

McIntyre, K. P., Mattingly, B. A., Lewandowski, G. W., & Simpson, A. (2014). Workplace self-expansion: Implications for job satisfaction, commitment, self-concept clarity, and self-esteem among the employed and unemployed. *Basic & Applied Social Psychology, 36*(14), 59-69. doi:10.1080/01973533.2013.856788

McKeown, E. (2010). Retention in the upswing. *T + D, 64*(3), 22. Retrieved from https://www.td.org

Meister, J. (2012, August). Job hopping is the 'new normal' for millennials: Three ways to prevent a human resource nightmare. *Forbes.* Retrieved from http://www.forbes.com

Meister, J. (2012, October). Three reasons you need to adopt a millennial mindset regardless of your age. *Forbes.* Retrieved from http://www.forbes.com

Milheim, K. L. (2012). Towards a better experience: Examining student needs in the online classroom through Maslow's hierarchy of needs model. *Journal of Online Learning and Teaching, 8*, 159. Retrieved from https://www.jolt.merlot.org

Moore, S. Y., Grunberg, L., & Krause, A. J. (2014). The relationship between work and home examination of white and blue-collar generational differences in a large U.S. organization. *Psychology, 5*, 1768-1776. doi:10.4236/psych.2014.515183

Moritz, B. (2014). How I did it... The U.S. chairman of PWC on keeping millennials engaged. *Harvard Business Review, 92*(11), 41-44. Retrieved from http://www.hbr.org

Moss, M., & Martins, N. (2014). Generational sub-cultures: Generation Y a sub-culture? *Mediterranean Journal of Social Sciences, 5*(21), 147-160.

doi:10.5901/mjss.2014.v5n21p147

Muscalu, E., & Muntean, S. (2013). Motivation: A stimulating factor for increasing human resource management performance. *Review of International Comparative Management/Revista De Management Comparat International, 14*, 303-309. Retrieved from http://www.rmci.ase.ro/

NAS Recruitment Innovation. (2014). *Recruiting & managing the generations.* Retrieved from http://www.nasrecruitment.com/

Ngima, W. M., & Kyongo, J. (2013). Contribution of motivational management to employee performance. *International Journal of Humanities and Social Science, 3*(14), 219-239. Retrieved from http://www.ijhssnet.com

Niaz, M. (2011). Pursuing self-interest or self-actualization? From capitalism to a steady-state, wisdom economy. *Ecological Economics, 70*, 577-584. doi:10.1016/j.ecolecon.2010.10.012

Nikravan, L. (2014, January). Gen Y: Big demands and high expectations. Retrieved from http://www2.deloitte.com

Nohria, N., Groysberg, B., & Lee, L. (2008). Employee motivation: A powerful new model. *Harvard Business Review, 86*(7-8), 78-86. Retrieved from http://www.hbr.org

Noltemeyer, A., Bush, K., Patton, J., & Bergen, D. (2012). The relationship among deficiency needs and growth needs: An empirical investigation of Maslow's theory. *Children and Youth Services Review, 34*, 1862-1867. doi:10.1016/j.childyouth.2012.05.021

O'Bannon, G. (2001). Managing our future: The Generation X factor. *Public Personnel Management, 30*, 95-109. doi:10.1177/009102600103000109

Okoro, E. A., & Washington, M. C. (2012). Workforce diversity and organizational communication: Analysis of human capital performance and productivity. *Journal of Diversity Management, 7*, 57-62. Retrieved from http://www. cluteinstitute.com/journals

Oladapo, V. (2014). The impact of talent management of retention. *Journal of Business Studies Quarterly, 5*(3), 19-36. Retrieved from http://www.jbsq.org

Olckers, C., & Plessis, Y. D. (2012). Psychological ownership: A managerial construct for talent retention and organisational effectiveness. *African Journal of Business Management, 6*, 2585-2596. doi:10.5897/AJBM.11.1018

Orth, U., Robins, R. W., & Widaman, K. F. (2012). Life-san development of self-esteem and its effects on important life outcomes. *Journal of Personality & Social Psychology, 102*, 1271-1288. doi:10.1037s0025558

Ozguner, Z., & Ozguner, M. (2014). A managerial point of view on the relationship between of Maslow's hierarchy of needs and Herzberg's dual factor theory. *International Journal of Business and Social Science, 5*(7), 207-215. Retrieved from http://www.ijbssnet.com/

Parijat , P., & Bagga , S. (2014). Victor Vroom's expectancy theory of motivation: An evaluation. *International Research Journal of Business and Management, 7*(9), 1-8. Retrieved from http://irjbm.org/

Parry, E., & Urwin, P. (2011). Generational differences in work values: A review of theory and evidence. *International Journal of Management Reviews, 13*, 79-96. doi:10.1111/j.1468-2370.2010.00285.x

Paulin, M., Ferguson, R. J., Jost, N., & Fallu, J. M. (2014). Motivating millennials to engage in charitable causes through social media. *Journal of Service Management, 25*, 334-348. doi:10.1108/JOSM-05-20-2013-0122

Pew Research Center. (2014, March 7). *Millennials in adulthood.* Retrieved from http://www.pewsocialtrends.org

Purohit, B., & Bandyopadhyay, T. (2014). Beyond job security and money: Driving factors of motivation for government doctors in India.

Human Resources for Health, 12, 1-26. doi:10.1186/1478-4491-12-12

Putre, L. (2013). Generations in the workplace. *Hospitals & Health Networks, 87,* 26-31. Retrieved from http://www.hhnmag.com

Ramli, M. S., & Jusoh, A. B. (2015). Expectancy theory analysis to conduct research at Malaysian Research University. *International Journal of Economics and Financial Issues, 5*(15), 1-7. Retrieved from http://www.econjournals.com

Renko, M., Kroeck, K. G., & Bullough, A. (2012). Expectancy theory and nascent entrepreneurship. *Small Business Economics, 39,* 667-684. doi:10.1007/s11187-011-9354-3

Rikleen, L. S. (2014). Where they're coming from. *Communication World, 31*(2), 14-17. Retrieved from http://cw.iabc.com

Roberts, K. (2012). The end of the long baby-boomer generation. *Journal of Youth Studies, 15,* 479-497. doi:10.1080/13676261.2012.663900

Rozuel, C. (2011). Transcending business ethics: Insights from Jung and Maslow. *Electronic Journal of Business Ethics and Organization Studies, 16,* 41-47. Retrieved from http://ejbo.jyu.fi

Saba, T. (2013, October 1). Understanding generational differences in the workplace: findings and conclusions. *Industrial Relations Centre (IRC) School of Policy Studies,*1-11. Retrieved from http://irc/queensu.ca

Sand, T., Cangemi, J., & Ingram, J. (2011). Say again? What do associates really want at work? *Organizational Development, 29,* 101-107. Retrieved from http://www.isodc.org

Saratovsky, K. D., & Feldmann, D. (2013). *Cause for change: The why and how of nonprofit millennial engagement.* San Francisco, CA: Jossey-Bass.

Schawbel, D. (2013, August 6). Millennial branding and Beyond.com survey reveals the rising cost of hiring workers from the millennial generation. Retrieved from http://millennialbranding.com/2013/cost-millennial-retention-study/

Schoch, T. (2012). Turning the ship around with a four-generation crew. *Information Management Journal, 46*(4), 25-29. Retrieved from http://www.ijim.in

Schullery, N. M. (2013). Workplace engagement and generational differences in values. *Business Communication Quarterly, 76*, 252-265. doi:10.1177/1080569913476543

Schultz, R. J., & Schwepker, C. H., Jr. (2012). Boomers vs. millennials: Critical conflict regarding sales culture, salesforce recognition, and supervisor expectations. *International Journal of Business, Humanities and Technology, 2*, 32-41. Retrieved from http://www.ijbhtnet.com

Schweitzer, E. S., & Lyons, S. T. (2010). New generation, great expectations: A field study of the millennial. *Journal of Business Psychology, 25*, 281-292. doi:10.1007/s10869-010-9159-4

Service Industry. (n.d.). *In Businessdictionary.com.* Retrieved from http://www.businessdictionary.com/definition/service-industry.html

Shragay, D., & Tziner, A. (2011). The generational effect on the relationship between job involvement, work satisfaction, and organizational citizenship behavior. *Revista de Psicologia del Trabajo y de las Organizaciones, 27*, 143-157. doi:10.5093/tr2011v27n2a6

Simon, M. (2011). *Dissertation and scholarly research: Recipes for success.* Seattle, WA: Dissertation Success.

Smith, D. B., & Shields, J. (2013). Factors related to social service workers' job satisfaction: Revisiting Herzberg's motivation to work. *Administration in Social Work, 37*, 189-198. doi:10.1080/03643107.2012.673217

Solnet, D., & Kralj, A. (2011). Generational differences in work attitudes:

Evidence from the hospitality industry. *FIU Hospitality Review, 29*(2), 37-54. Retrieved from http://digitalcommons.fiu.edu/hospitalityreview/

Soulez, C. G., & Soulez, S. (2014). On the heterogeneity of Generation Y job preferences. *Employee Relations, 36*, 319-332. doi:10.1108/ER-07-2013-0073

Sterling, A., & Boxall, P. (2013). Lean production, employee learning, and workplace outcomes: A case analysis through the ability-motivation-opportunity framework. *Human Resource Management Journal, 23*, 227-240. doi:10.1111/1748-8583.12010

Stowe, B. (2013, March 9). What impact will millennials have on the workplace? Retrieved from http://research.gigaom.com

Sultan, S. (2012). Examining the job characteristics: A matter of employee's work motivation and job satisfaction. *Journal of Behavioural Sciences, 22*(2), 13-25. Retrieved from http://jab.sagepub.com

Sundriyal, R., & Kumar, R. (2014). Happiness and wellbeing. *International Journal of Indian Psychology, 4*(2), 19-27. Retrieved from https://www.ijip.in

Tang, T. L., Cunningham, P. H., Frauman, E., & Perry, T. L. (2012). Attitudes and occupational commitment among public personnel: Differences between baby boomers and Gen-Xers. *Public Personnel, 41*, 327-360. doi:10.1177/009102601204100206

Taormina, R. J., & Gao, J. H. (2013). Maslow and the motivation hierarchy: Measuring satisfaction of the needs. *American Journal of Psychology, 126*, 155-177. doi:10.5406/amerijpsyc.126.2.0155

Taylor, P. (2014). *The next America: Boomers, millennials, and the looming generational showdown.* New York, NY: Public Affairs.

Thomas, S. G. (2011, July 9). The divorce generation. *Wall Street Journal.* Retrieved from http://wsj.com

Thompson, C., & Gregory, J. B. (2012). Managing millennials: A framework for improving attraction, motivation, and retention. *The Psychologist-Manager Journal, 15*, 237-246. doi:10.1080/10887156.2012.730444

Tillman, A. (2013). Improving worker satisfaction yields improved worker-retention rates. *Employment Relations Today, 39*(4), 27-31. doi:10.1002/ert.21386

Trefalt, S. (2013). Between you and me: Setting work-nonwork boundaries in the context of workplace relationships. *Academy of Management Journal, 56*, 1802-1829. doi:10.5465/amj.2011.0298

Tuch, A. N., & Hornbaek, K. (2015). Does Herzberg's notion of hygienes and motivators apply to user experience? *ACM Transactions on Computer-Human Interaction, 22*(4), 16:1-16:25. doi:10.1145/2724710

Tulgan, B. (2009). *Not everyone gets a trophy: How to manage Generation Y.* San Francisco, CA: Jossey-Bass.

Tulgan, B. (2013, October). How to bring out the best in today's talent. *Professional Safety, 58*(10), 38-40. Retrieved from http://www.asse.org/professional-safety/

Twenge, J., Campbell, W., & Freeman, E. (2012). Generational differences in young adults' life goals, concern for others, and civic orientation, 1966-2009. *Journal of Personality and Social Psychology, 102*, 1045-1062. doi:10.1037/a0027408

Udechukwu, I. (2009). Correctional officer turnover: Of Maslow's needs hierarchy and Herzberg motivation theory. *Public Personnel Administration & Public Personnel Review, 38*(2), 69-82. doi:10.1177/009102600903800205

Van der Heijden, G. A., Schepers, J. J., & Nijssen, E. J. (2012). Understanding workplace boredom among white-collar employees: Temporary reactions and individual differences. *European Journal of Work and Organizational Psychology, 21*, 349-375.

doi:10.1080/1359432x.2011.578824

VanMeter, R., Grisaffe, D., Chonko, L., & Roberts, J. (2013). Generation Y's ethical ideology and its potential workplace implications. *Journal of Business Ethics, 117*, 93-109. doi:10.1007/s10551-012-1505-1

Venter, H. J. (2012). Maslow's self-transcendence: How it can enrich organization culture and leadership. *International Journal of Business, Humanities and Technology, 2*(7), 64-71. Retrieved from http://www.ijbhtnet.com/

Verschoor, C. C. (2013). Ethical behavior differs among generations. *Strategic Finance, 95*(8), 11-14. Retrieved from http://www.imanet.org

Vroom, R. H. (1964). *Work and motivation.* New York, NY: John Wiley & Sons.

Ware, B. L. (2014). Stop the GEN Y revolving door. *T + D, 68*(5), 58-63. Retrieved from https://www.td.org/Publications/Magazines/TD

Wendling, W. (2012). The relationship between incentives to learn and Maslow's hierarchy of needs. *International Conference of Applied Physics and Industrial Engineering, 24*(B), 1335-1342. doi:10.1016/j.phpro.2012.02.199

Young, S. J., Sturts, J. R., Ross, C. M., & Kim, K. T. (2013). Generational differences and job satisfaction in leisure services. *Managing Leisure, 18*, 152-170. doi:10.1080/13606719.2013.752213

Zhong, C. B., & House, J. (2012). Hawthorne revisited: Organizational implications of the physical work environment. *Research in Organizational Behavior, 32*, 3-22. doi:10.1016/j.riob.2012.10.004

Zopiatis, A., Kapardis, M. K., & Varnavas, A. (2012). Y-ers, X-ers, and boomers: Investigating the multigenerational (mis) perceptions in the hospitality workplace. *Tourism and Hospitality Research, 12*(2),101-121. doi:10.1177/1467358412466668

www.ingramcontent.com/pod-product-compliance
Lightning Source LLC
Chambersburg PA
CBHW030650220526
45463CB00005B/1713